Farther Up the Main

Copyright © 2010 Wayne J. Lutz

1st Edition printed 2010: ISBN 978-0-9781357-6-8

All rights reserved. No part of this publication may be reproduced, stored in a retrieval system, or transmitted, in any form or by any means, electronic, mechanical, photocopying, recording, or otherwise, without the written prior permission of the author. Reviewers are authorized to quote short passages within a book review, as permitted under the United States Copyright Act of 1976.

Note for Librarians: a catalog record for this book that includes Dewey Decimal Classification and U.S. Library of Congress numbers is available from the Library and Archives of Canada. The complete catalog record can be obtained from their online database at:
www.collectionscanada.ca/amicus/index-e.html

ISBN 978-0-9781357-6-8
Printed in the United States of America

Powell River Books
Powell River BC, Canada
Book sales online at:
www.powellriverbooks.com
phone: 604-483-1704
email: wlutz@mtsac.edu

10 9 8 7 6 5 4 3 2 1

Farther Up the Main
Coastal British Columbia Stories

Wayne J. Lutz

2010
Powell River Books

To Dave Hodgins...

For his prominent leadership of the Powell River ATV Club and his significant contributions to the next generation of BC off-road riders

The stories are true, and the characters are real. All of the mistakes rest solely with the author.

Other Books by Wayne J. Lutz

Coastal British Columbia Stories

Up the Lake
Up the Main
Up the Winter Trail
Up the Strait
Up the Airway
Farther Up the Lake
Farther Up the Strait

Science Fiction Titles

Echo of a Distant Planet
Inbound to Earth

Front Cover Photo:
Climbing out of Theodosia Valley

Back Cover Photos:
Top – Mount Mahony
Bottom – Khartoum Lake

Acknowledgements

Powell River Books, a small publishing company, relies on a few key individuals to support this author's writing projects. My steadfast editor is Margy Lutz, who reviews my chapters more times than any prisoner-of-print should endure. John Maithus, without even trying, contributes topics for stories that will occupy my chapters for decades. And Bro teaches me how to relax.

Wayne J. Lutz
Powell River, British Columbia
August 10, 2010

Contents

Preface – After *Up the Main* 10
1 – April Snow 12
2 – Mount Alfred 27
3 – Boys' Night Out 50
4 – Theodosia 67
5 – Rain Turnin' to Snow 83
6 – Pickin' Apples 95
Center-of-Book Photos 107
7 – Heather Main 111
8 – Khartoum 132
9 – Granite Lake 6 144
10 – Cabin Huntin' 155
11 – Mount Mahony 177
12 – Last Chance 186
Epilogue – Outdoors 206
Geographic Index 208

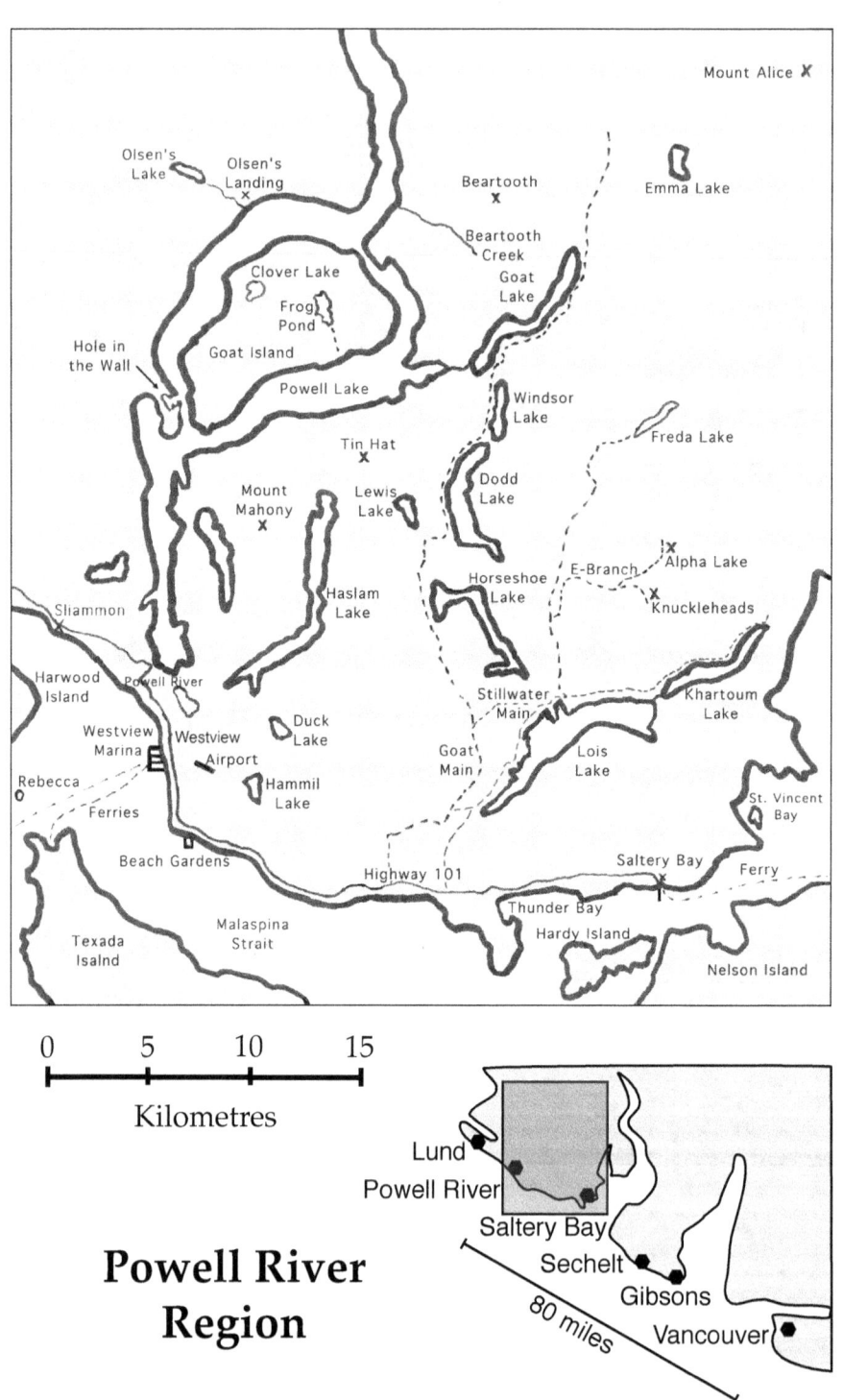

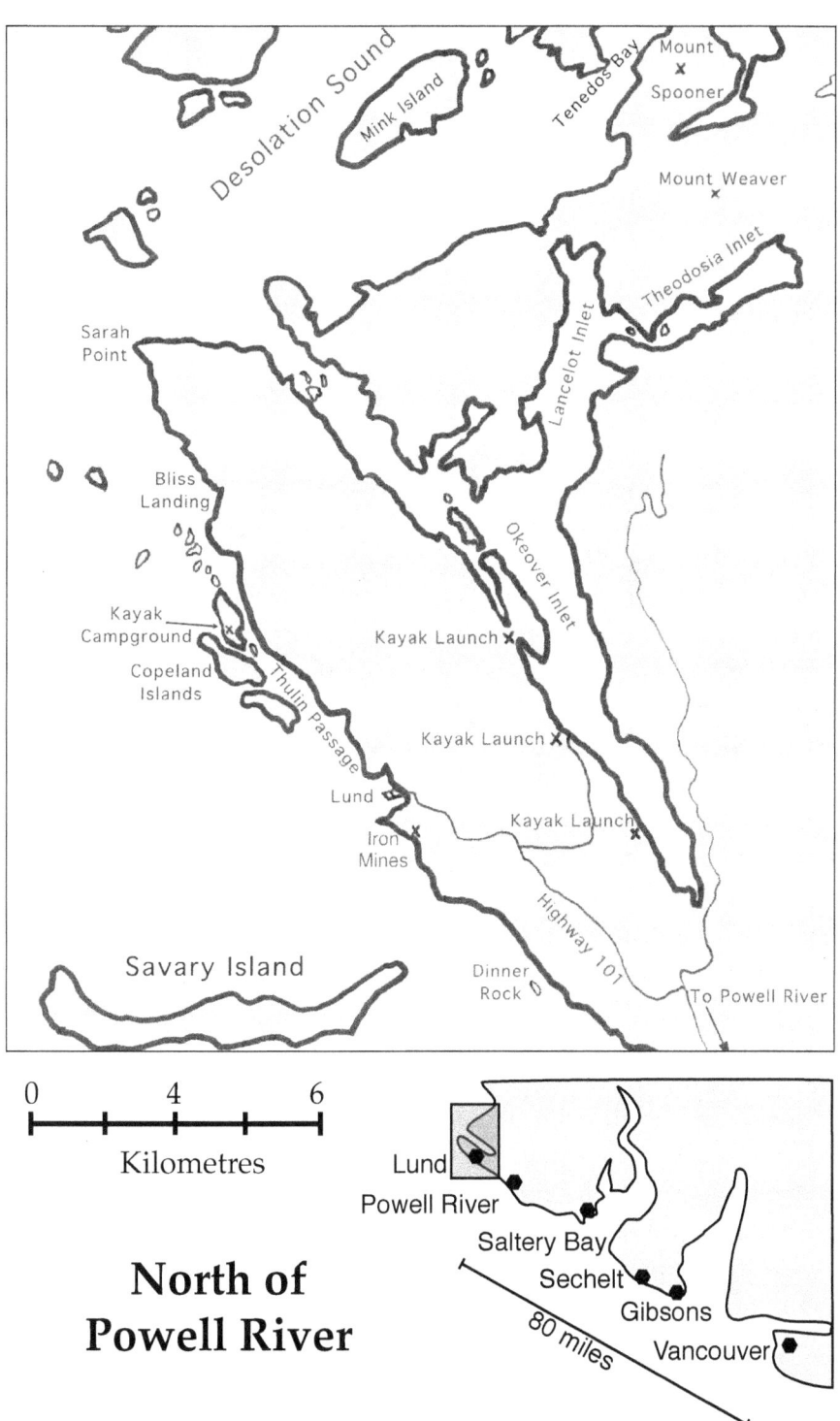

Preface

After *Up the Main*

One of my first books in the series *Coastal British Columbia Stories* focused on quad riding and my outsider-looking-in viewpoints regarding the backcountry surrounding Powell River. At the time, I envisioned *Up the Main* as an interesting topic for a book, rather than a personal life-long adventure. As I viewed it, learning to ride a quad and exploring the local region was a fine sport for those interested in such exploits, but I didn't see it as an activity that would hold my interest over time.

I thought that taking a few quad rides would allow me to experience a unique form of recreation that's a passion to some, write a book that should appeal to locals, and then turn to other pursuits. Little did I know I would become addicted.

During that first ride with John on a quad rented from his cousin, I thrashed through some challenging paths, and came to appreciate the physical effort demanded on the trail. Riding with John was a step above a typical introductory trip, but he went easy on me. When I balked at buying a quad, he convinced me that a small (100 cc) motorcycle would be enough to get started, particularly since he knew motorcycles intrigued me more than quads. The small motorcycle proved inadequate for many routes, both because of the limitations of the bike and my weak riding skills. But it appealed to my sense of adventure, and I began to ride for all of the right reasons.

At first, riding the motorbike was a full-time job, so I missed a lot of the natural surroundings. Even glancing beyond the side of the road was a nerve-wracking chore. But slowly, I gained in riding skills, and began to take in the amazing scenery, not just when I stopped, but even as I rode.

My wife, Margy, was willing to give off-road riding a try, but the motorcycle option wasn't her forte. Instead, she settled on a 250 cc two-wheel drive quad, enough to get her started. Off we'd go – me on my wimpy 100 cc motorcycle, Margy on her 250 cc bike, and John (with Bro in his aft box) on a bruising 660 cc quad. John's patience was often tested, but we made it through the introductory stage, and soon both Margy and I were hooked.

Today, Margy and I ride 450 cc quads, but we still prefer to follow John when we venture out. There's nothing like a ride with him to discover new places and tackle exploits you'd never try on your own. He knows how to push us to the limit, but not quite make us break. And these days, Margy and I even venture out on our own, tracing trails on maps, following routes recommended by friends, and exploring side-spurs that go to places unknown. We may not be experienced riders, but we're appreciative ones. And rides are no longer undertaken just to write another chapter. There's more to it than that – it's now a life-long pursuit.

Over the past three years, since the publication of *Up the Main*, I've ventured farther into the bush and occasionally even more boldly. But you don't have to be fearless to enjoy off-road travel to new destinations or places you enjoy revisiting again and again. Thus, the word "Farther" in *Farther Up the Main* represents a journey in both distance and attitude. What I once expected to be a passing fancy is now an integral part of my life. It's proof positive that it's not just the destination that's important – it's how you get there.

Chapter 1

April Snow

Under a showery early evening sky, the blue-and-white Campion floats in "fishing position" within First Narrows, engine off. Her bow bobs near the rock cliff a few metres from the green navigation marker. For the first time this year, the front and rear canvas are unsnapped and pulled half-aside, while the top canvas provides protection from the intermittent sprinkles. The center windshield is hinged open and the overhead canvas hatch is unzipped and thrown back, allowing walk-through access to the bow. I haven't removed all the canvas yet, since it still looks like rain, but it's only sprinkling at the moment. In this configuration, I have easy access to the two best fishing locations in opposite ends of the boat. Sometimes, as the boat drifts, I move from bow to stern with my line still out, sliding my rod over the top canvas from one outstretched hand to the other. It's a long reach, but it keeps my lure in the water without interruption.

I've fished for two hours in the fading light on this second day of April, one day after the opening of trout season on the lake. Everything in nature seems about three weeks late this spring, even the fish. So far, I've seen one small trout follow my line to the boat, but no strikes on my red-and-white daredevil. The birds and wildflowers seem equally delayed by the unusually prolonged winter. Today, nearly two full weeks into official spring, it's barely acceptable to remove the canvas from the Campion, but I'm defiant. If spring hasn't sprung, maybe I can hurry it up a bit.

John and Rick have been defiant, too. They arrived at Hole in the Wall mid-day for a hike along the logging roads and the spur trails bordering Chippewa Bay. When John and Rick pulled into the Hole this morning, John swung his Hourston in a wide arc towards my cabin – *Hello!* – before veering off to the other side of the bay. As the boat's wake spread in a curve, Bro stuck his head out the back of the overhead canvas, preparing for arrival at one of his favourite cabins. I returned their greeting from my cabin deck with a wide wave of my arm, a few seconds too late to be seen by anybody but the black Lab.

As soon as John's boat pulled to a stop at Cabin Number 2 and the engine went silent, I shouted "Hey, guys!" across the bay while watching two men and a dog in my binoculars.

John's return holler was simple, his words clipped to assure I heard him across the bay: "Hey, Wayne! We're goin' hikin'." The two brothers and the black dog quickly climbed the cliffside stairs, with only a brief pause as John gave Bro a needed ass-push up the final rock ledge. They disappeared into the trees and were gone – six hours ago.

Now I float in First Narrows, a bit worried. Both John and Rick are sturdy hikers, but they like to push it. There's little doubt where they've gone – down the steepest trails to Chippewa as far as they can: "Let's see if we can get farther than last time, and find something new."

Even more likely, they are working on the trail to the new steam donkey, which is "new" only in the sense it's the most recent "old" steam donkey John has found in this area. Hikes into this thick logging area aren't unusual. What isn't normal is the time. It's now approaching sunset, and John and Rick will need to get down the lake before it gets dark. They are careful about pushing darkness, especially when it includes a boat trip back down the lake, and already it seems past their limit.

To the west, above Chippewa Bay, a thick mist of snow has been falling for the last two hours, a constant wall of gray-white. If John or Rick slips and falls or even twists an ankle in this backcountry, it'll be a formidable hike back to the Hole. An unscheduled overnight stay in this area, although not deadly for these guys, would be far from comfortable.

Already my imagination has taken over: "Hey, Doug, get my motorcycle from the storage shed at the condo, and meet me at the Shinglemill at 6 am. We'll use my boat to bring the bike to Number 2, and then we'll rope it up the cliff. One of us can ride up the main to find them, while the other stands by the phone." I rehearse the rescue plan in my mind.

I hear the sound of the Hourston's Yamaha four-stroke only moments before it charges around the corner from Hole in the Wall and out into First Narrows. John targets my boat immediately, aims his Hourston directly at my bobbing position, and immediately comes off-plane to glide up against my bow. The Campion is pointing straight at the Hourston, so I flick my docking lights on and then off quickly: *Hello!* My rescue plans aren't needed.

As usual, John times his arrival perfectly, the Hourston drifting right up to me in a perfect raft-up maneuver. He gives the outboard a quick spurt of reverse, and comes to a halt within arm's reach. I stand in the front of my boat with my fishing rod, while John reaches through his open side window for my bow. He turns off his engine, and as if on cue, it begins to pour.

"How was the steam donkey?" I ask.

"You guessed it," replies John. "We worked on the trail some more. We've got to get you up there soon, before the new logging road is finished and messes it up."

John is used to spending days working on a trail that's obliterated a few weeks later.

"Lot of snow right now," says Rick, "and it's coming down pretty good up there today. But the trail's in nice shape."

"Any fish?" says John.

"Caught seven so far."

"Yeah, right. April fool to you too," says Rick. "It's still too cold, even for the trout."

The rain is pouring down in sheets now, and I'm standing in the bow getting soaked. My jacket, hat, and snow pants provide some protection, but this is ridiculous.

"Get out of the rain," says John as he reaches out of his window and pushes off my bow. He starts his engine and backs away. By now we've both drifted nearly into the middle of the channel.

"Hey, can you take me riding tomorrow?" I yell as the Hourston slowly retreats.

"Sure, if the weather holds. But it looks like snow, even here."
"In April?"
"Why not? Winter isn't over yet."
He's right, and the fish know it.

* * * * *

When I get back to my cabin, I'm totally drenched. The rain stopped just as suddenly as it began, and now the western sky is a mix of blue and pink, with stunning white clouds catching the evening sunset. I contemplate leaving the canvas off the bow and stern, but it could rain again tonight. So I take the time to button up the boat. For the moment, I give in to the delayed arrival of spring.

* * * * *

The next morning, I awaken to my alarm and two inches of new snow. If I'd left the boat covers open, it would've been a mess for my trip to town. So I luck out with a dry boat beneath the canvas. By 7 am, the

Campion is loaded and ready to go. If I get going early enough, I can be ready to ride before John wakes up. Since he's always rushing me, it would be fun to be ahead of schedule, and to rush him for a change. But there's lots to do first, including the boat ride to the Shinglemill, the drive to town, a quick check for email at the condo, dressing in clothes appropriate for riding, breakfast, and getting the quad trailer hitched up at the airport hangar.

The trip down the lake is a sublime ride. In all directions, new snow covers the mountains. The sky is mostly clear, with the rising sun still hidden behind Goat Island to the east. The lake is smooth, making the morning flotsam easy to spot, so I can drive at a comfortable 40 klicks.

I hustle through my morning chores in town and pull up in back of John's house shortly after 9 am. There's no place to park. The entire area is clogged with Ed's van, Rick's taxicab, both of John's trucks (his "new" one torn apart on the lawn for renovation), and Rick's pickup. I manage to park straddling the driveway and jutting out into the alley.

Bro runs out to greet me, so I know the household is awake. But I notice John's quad isn't yet loaded in his truck, so I'm still ahead of schedule. The downstairs door is unlocked, so I walk in and yell up the stairs to John: "Hey, man, let's get going. I don't have all day."

Helen comes down the stairs, smiling and chuckling in her normal jovial mood: "John's still eating breakfast. He isn't ready yet."

"Well, he'd better hurry up," I reply.

Helen laughs; she knows John is typically impatient with my dawdling.

"Hey, John!" Helen yells up the stairs. "Wayne's ready to go. You'd better get movin'."

"In a minute!" is John's disgusted reply.

Never mess with John when he's eating.

* * * * *

The potholed road along the south edge of Haslam Lake brings me to a crawl. My red Kodiak 450 rides alone on a two-quad trailer behind my truck (Margy's truck, appropriately hijacked for this occasion). In the side mirrors, I watch the rig bouncing excessively, even at this slow speed. I hope the axle stays in one piece. Once in a while, I catch a glimpse of the quad jostling on the trailer, fighting its restraining straps. The winter has taken a toll on this dirt road, and the ride is rough all the way from Duck Lake to our off-loading spot near Mud Lake.

In front of me, John's old truck, with its completely worn-out shocks, plods forward at my same slow pace. The blue Grizzly 660 in the Ford's bed sways from side-to-side. Bro's nose pokes out of the passenger window, taking in the familiar sights and sniffing for bear.

Near Duck Lake, I spot two deer in a logging slash along the side of the road, so I stop to watch. One of the deer is positioned next to a stump, its hooves on top, standing on its hind legs. From my viewpoint, it seems to be standing at a lunch counter, waiting to be served. In that position, the deer looks like a kangaroo without a long tail. Finally, after both deer stare at me without moving, I continue down the road. I find John pulled off in a turnout, waiting for me.

"Trouble with the trailer?" he asks.

"No, just two very unusual things."

"What?"

"A deer standing on a stump, looking like a kangaroo."

John laughs: "Sounds kinda funny. What was the other thing?"

"Deer alongside the road that you didn't see."

John's eyesight is so much better than mine that I never see anything before he does.

"Must not have been there when I passed by."

John's explanation isn't meant to challenge me; it's mere logic.

* * * * *

At our off-load spot near Mud Lake, I unfasten the straps from my quad and drive it off the trailer as quickly as I can, trying to stay ahead of John. So far, I'm winning, but it never lasts for long. By the time I slip into my rain gear and pull on my full-face mask, John is already off-loaded, sitting on his quad, helmet on, and waiting for me. Bro is aboard in his aft box, wearing his blue sweater and matching raincoat, also ready to go. I stuff my backpack and riding gear into the cargo box on the back of my quad and try to scrunch my lunch bag on top, but I can't close the lid.

"Can you take my lunch?" I ask.

"Sure, strap it on front," says John. "You've got to learn to pack light."

He's right, but I like to have all the extras on every trip. Besides, there's always room for a bit more on John's bike.

"I'm finally ready," I announce, as I climb on my quad.

John starts his engine and is out of sight down the dirt road before I can engage my starter. Finally I'm on my way, but before I make it to the first bridge, I have to turn back. I don't want to delay John any longer, but I've forgotten something essential – my heavy gloves. I'm wearing my fingerless gloves, which won't be nearly enough today.

"Now what?" asks John when I pull up beside him where he has been waiting for me at an intersection.

"Forgot my gloves. Had to go back," I confess.

John's unsympathetic reply: "Oh."

After riding a short distance, the road veers to the right, up the route known as the Alaska Pine. This trail is one of my favourites, and our tracks today are the first in the fresh snow. John has found a new (meaning "old") trail to a lookout near the top of the Alaska Pine, and he's been clipping alders lately to make it passable. He's not sure I'll be able to handle the steep slope, particularly in the snow, but he's willing to let me give it a try. I'm not the most aggressive rider, but I'm up for the challenge.

As we begin our climb up the Alaska Pine, John leads on his Grizz, celebrating the fresh snow by fishtailing from side to side when the trail occasionally flattens. Bro sticks his head out to the side of his aft box, like a dog sticking his nose out the window of a zooming car.

This trail has the unique feel of true off-road riding, climbing steeply into the forest, but well within my capabilities. It provides a sense of stretching my limits without exceeding them. There's just something about the Alaska Pine (*Up the Winter Trail*, Chapter 4).

We pause at a lookout that gives us a view of the northern stretch of Haslam Lake. John points out the high cliff that's our goal – the end

of his new-old trail. It's a spot that seems unreachable, but John hiked there on-foot several years ago from the road paralleling the shoreline of Haslam Lake. The footpath is an impossible route for a quad or motorcycle, so he decided to try to approach the cliff from above. He calls it the "Five-Day Trail," since it took five days for him to reopen the old logging road with the help of Rick and a friend.

As we climb the Alaska Pine, the lead rider (John) faces the toughest job. An endless line of snow-laden bushes and small trees confronts him. After last night's storm, they droop across the trail, blocking our path. Each hanging branch needs only a quick tug before it leaps skyward and out of our way. But the rider beneath is hit by snow flung back down. Bro hates this process, since he receives the brunt of the tumbling snow. For smaller branches, John simply rubs against them with his arm or lets them bump harmlessly against his helmet. Bigger branches require a stop-and-tug to release them of their snowy load. Bro rides patiently in his aft box, waiting to be whacked by the next limb that sneaks by John.

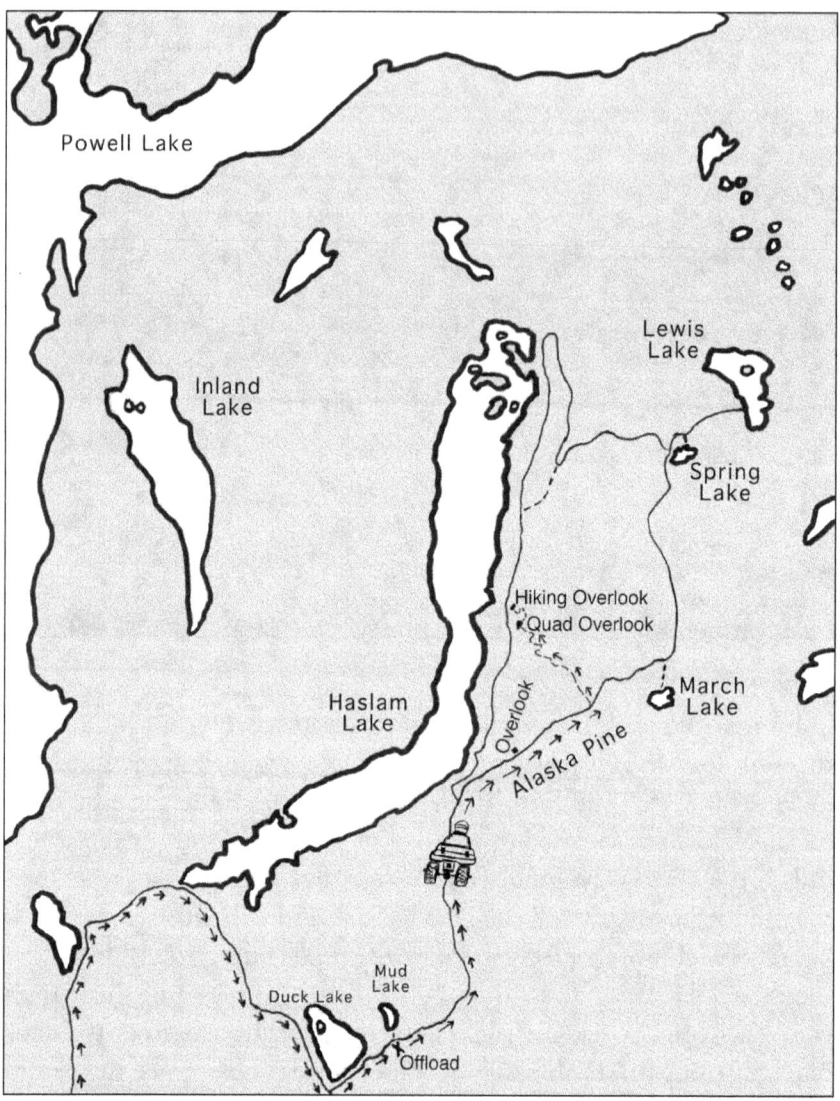

I watch John and Bro getting smacked by branches and covered in snow. Bro's black head becomes a black-and-white helmet of snow and fur. After a kilometre of this, I pull up next to John at a wide spot in the trail.

"Can I lead for a while?" I ask. "I'll knock down the snow for us."

John's quick reply is: "Sure, you can lead."

This is an unexpected response from a guy who always leads on rides. I'm pleased he'll allow me to take care of some of the drudgery for a change. He's used to doing whatever it takes to get me to my destination, and that normally means a lot of work, including being thumped by branches and pummeled with snow.

I take the lead and whack a few branches. But almost as soon as I move out in front, the trail changes to a wide-open path, with few overhanging limbs. After another half-kilometre, I pull to the side and wait for John to join me.

"I took over at a good time," I say. "There aren't many low-hanging branches through here."

"I know," replies John. "That's why I let you lead, but it was nice of you to offer."

"Oh."

John takes back the lead, and we turn off the Alaska Pine onto the Five-Day Trail. At first we start downhill, riding easily through one-foot deep water in a muddy flow of rust-coloured rocks and small, tumbling cascades that turn the trail into a temporary stream.

John stops in the middle of the gushing water and yells back to me when I pull up behind him:

"You can lead for a while now. You'll have lots of branches to swamp you with snow, so go slow. This part of the trail is an easy ride – mostly level or slightly downhill – an old logging road, so it was easy to reactivate."

I maneuver around him, and start down the beautiful trail. In fact, in all of my travels on a quad, it's one of the most majestic paths I've seen. Occasional pockets of old-growth firs and cedars are mixed with closely spaced second-growth trees. John points out one particularly large pine. White pine, with its long blue-green needles is rare in this area.

At one point, John shows me a tree growing out of the trunk of another, a twisted mass of wood. I stop to take a picture, but it's difficult to capture this contorted jumble in a photo.

I whack through the snowy bushes arching in from both sides of the trail. When I pull on bigger branches to launch them upward, I'm blasted with snow. It builds up on my quad and covers my entire body.

My helmet is plastered. I pull my snow-covered goggles down and let them hang around my neck.

John lets me lead for nearly a kilometre. After this easy-to-ride path, the trail climbs steeply upward. During the trail-building process, this secton required lots of work. John has told me I'll need to use my "lockers" here. I've used them only once in an aborted attempt to climb out of Suicide Creek (*Up the Winter Trail*, Chapter 12). Differential lockers are notorious for getting you through the tough stuff, even better than four-wheel-drive, but they make steering difficult.

Before beginning the climb, I pull to the side of the trail so John can get by. My quad is encased in white from its frequent dowsing, so I get off and begin to push the snow from my quad. John stops me.

"Leave it on the front. It'll help keep your weight forward during the climb. It's pretty steep."

John even adds some more snow to the front rack of my quad and packs it down, while I push the snow off my seat and the rear of the bike. He gives me some simple instructions on how to drive my Kodiak up this steep part of the trail.

"Give 'er shit, and don't let up, or its over."

Simple and to the point.

I can do this. But the first hill ahead looks mighty steep. Narrow too, with trees on each side to pose a steering challenge with my lockers engaged.

John lifts Bro out of his box, letting him walk up the hill. When he does this, you know the trail is about to get tough. I can only see a small portion of the slope ahead, as it winds to the left and out of sight. The part I see seems to fit within my personal limits, so I'm ready to give it a try.

John drives his quad forward to the base of the hill, and I move ahead to position my bike behind his. Immediately, my undercarriage lodges firmly on a small stump sticking up in the center of the trail. I shift into reverse, but still can't move.

John gets off his bike and walks back to assist: "That's the same stump where Rick got stuck," he says without a hint of concern.

So far, I've traveled only a metre on this difficult section of the trail, and I'm already stuck. I haven't even started up the hill yet.

"You'll need to get off so we can move your quad," says John. "Keep it in reverse and add a little power."

We lift and rock the quad, while I push the thumb-throttle, and the bike finally moves backwards off the stump.

"Okay, now I'm ready," I declare. "I'll get serious this time."

John laughs and walks back to his quad. He launches up the hill, lockers engaged and engine roaring, snow and mud flying out from his tracks as he rounds the corner and out of sight. A few seconds later, I hear his quad engine return to idle. He's ready for me to give it a try.

Up I go. I lean forward on the steepest spots, which makes steering difficult with the lockers. My thumb momentarily slips from the throttle, but I recover quickly, gunning the engine. When I reach a straighter and less steep stretch of trail, I sit back for a moment to recoup my energy for the next climbing turn. There is one more forward-leaning climb, and then I'm past the hardest part. John waits on his quad at the crest of the hill, twisted around to watch the show.

"Right on!" he yells. "Good job!"

Coming from him, I take it as the ultimate compliment. But I'm sure he heard my momentary release of the throttle, so I'd better confess.

"My thumb fell off the throttle for a second," I admit. "I was having a hard time steering with the lockers and keeping the throttle forward at the same time. I'll do better on the next section."

John nods his head approvingly, without even deducting a point for the slipped throttle. I now realize he really thought this trail was beyond my capability, and he's glad to see I'll be okay. With his help, I've come a long way.

Several more steep hills follow, all conquered easier than the first. Then we start down a gentle winding grade, followed by one final tough climb, and we are there.

We break out into the sun on a wide swath of snow-covered granite overlooking Haslam Lake. To the south, we can see the Blue Ridge overlook where John has taken me before. Below us, the logging road winds along Haslam. It's a magnificent view.

We take a well-deserved break, while Bro barks at eagles soaring near the cliff. The more he barks, the closer they come, as if to taunt him. Finally, Bro settles down, stretching out in the snow for a rest.

"Only jack pines here," says John. "Too dry for anything else."

The evergreens in this region are mostly fir, cedar, and hemlock, with only a few pines and spruce, and that's fortunate for us. The bark beetle is closing in from the north, closer each year, devastating the pine forests along the way. The loss is immeasurable, but most of our local trees will be spared.

After we eat our lunch and relax a few minutes, John asks me if I'm willing to try to hike to a spot where there is another cliff with an even better view of the lake. It's less than a kilometre from here, and it's the spot he originally reached years ago, hiking up from the logging road far below.

Slogging through the forest in rocky areas covered with snow takes a lot of energy. I'm sweating beneath my multi-layers of clothing. In a few hundred metres we find a faded piece of red trail marking tape, then another.

"Old tape," says John. "From the hiking trail that comes up from the main."

It's hard to imagine how anyone could've hiked all this way from the logging road on a nearly vertical slope.

"Just a little farther," says John. "I remember this part of the trail. See, there's an old log I cut to get through here."

Not only did he hike all the way up from the lake, he carried his chain saw with him.

Bro bounds ahead of us, acting like he remembers the way to the viewpoint. Sunlight begins to stream through the trees ahead, and there it is – an even more magnificent vista than the end of the quad trail. This view is from the highest edge of the cliff. Bro plops down in the snow, and John sits with him on the ledge, looking out over Haslam Lake.

A light westerly breeze pushes air against the cliff and up towards us. In the swirling air from below, mist drifts upward, forming small clouds right in front of us. Clouds must begin somewhere, and this is one of those places.

I look southwest, seeing the northern half of Texada Island and the mountains of Vancouver Island beyond. Farther north sits Mount Mahony, Tin Hat, Goat Island, Beartooth, and the high country beyond Powell Lake. It's a glorious day in the early April sun. We sit on the edge of the cliff, snow lying in patches nearby. Towering cumulus clouds surround our perch, billowing upward in the warming air. Spring cannot be far behind.

Chapter 2

Mount Alfred

John has talked about Ice Lake for months. Last year, during the summer, local trail builders began pushing through on their quads from the north end of Goat Lake, trying to reach an area previously accessible only by strenuous hiking. Quad teams with picks and shovels have breached several landslides on the old logging road, but bigger vehicles can't get through. Trucks with trail-building tools must be parked short of the landslides, with equipment shuttled in on quads. By the time snow shuts down efforts for the winter, a quad trail has been reopened to the third stream. Beyond this creek lies a challenging hike over a footbridge to Ice Lake.

Ice Lake is the current end point for a route leading towards Jervis Inlet. Beyond the lake, the terrain is too precipitous to even consider a quad trail (yet), although there has been reassuring talk by local entrepreneurs regarding a future public road to Squamish along this same path. Such a route would continue from Ice Lake, along the south slope of Mount Alfred, down to the head of Jervis Inlet. Not in my lifetime, I hope.

The following spring, a local group begins trail building again, finishing the bridge at the second major creek. The first stream, nicknamed Spray Creek, is fordable, but it's not a permanent solution. Stream protection requires a bridge, a level of sophistication not yet possible considering the financial funding for the project – zero dollars. The third rush of water is still too strong to get across, but that will change as the summer dries it to a creekbed crossing. In short order, a bridge will span this creek, but the final trail to Ice Lake will remain a footpath for a long time.

In early June, landslides closed the logging road, worsened by the damaging blow-downs of the previous winter. Quads can make it through, but not trucks. The BOMB Squad (Bloody Old Men's Brigade) has volunteered its efforts to assist with improving the trail to Ice Lake, but they need to get their trucks past the landslides. John takes the battle to heart.

He visits the local office of Western Forest Products, a regional logging company, to discuss the problem. When I hear this, I cringe. John in a logging office is like a Grit at a Conservative political rally. Nothing can come of it except trouble. But he reports his visit went well, with the logging office promising to assist with clearing the landslides so hikers can access a trailhead to Ice Lake. They could use some photos of the landslides as ammunition. John volunteers me.

I've looked forward to my first quad ride to this area and the hike to Ice Lake, so taking a few pictures isn't too high a price. But how John deals with the photos in the confines of the logging office could be – scratch the political analogy – like a bull in a china shop.

We decide to take only one truck, with John's Grizzly in the back of his Ford and my Kodiak on the trailer. To keep the quad ride within fuel limits, we'll drive farther than normal in the truck. The round-trip on our quads will be reduced to a reasonable 70 kilometres.

We probably won't be able to make it all the way to Ice Lake, since the final trail will be crowded with overhanging alders. Besides, without a quad trail to get farther than the third creek, we'll likely run out of time and energy. Still, I retain hope we'll make it to the lake. With lots of sunlit hours this time of year, it's not impossible.

* * * * *

When I pull into the alley behind John's house, John's old truck is already hooked to my trailer, my Kodiak sitting on top. What luxury – John has already picked up the trailer and my quad at the airport, so we're ready to go.

Blocking the rest of the driveway is Doug's blue pickup with his quad wedged under its fiberglass canopy, tailgate open to support the rear wheels. This is my first indication Doug is riding with us today. I'm glad – he's a likeable fellow with a vast knowledge of the wilderness. His long blond dreadlocks and Oakland Raiders pants, along with his thick New Zealand accent, distinguish him from your typical quad rider.

As I greet Doug and John, Ed sticks his head out of the upstairs window. I expect some kind of here-comes-trouble greeting.

"Motley looking crew. You'd better take along your author's notebook," he says.

"Got it!" I say, pulling a little blue spiral notebook from my pocket. I flip it open and poise myself with pen in hand: "Would you give me some words of wisdom before we depart?"

"Do you have a will?" he asks.

I pretend to scribble in my notebook. I'll remind Ed when I return from this trip that it was he who jinxed us.

"Don't need one," I reply. "It's always an easier and slower ride when John has a bad back."

Doug laughs because he understands. No one pushes trail building harder than John. He can't lead even a simple ride without needing to prune the forest. But he's recovering from a strained back, so I figure we might get away with less work today.

Doug pulls away in his truck, to meet us near Windsor Lake. I extract my camera from my backpack and ask Ed to catch it when I toss it up to him on the balcony. In its thickly padded bag, the camera faces a short, safe toss, but I stand ready to catch it if it falls from Ed's hands. He makes a good catch, snaps a photo of John and me, and drops the camera back down.

"Might be your last picture," says Ed.

"Stop it," I say.

As we climb aboard John's truck, I notice there's a pry-bar and sledgehammer strapped to the front of my quad. Maybe John's back isn't so bad after all.

* * * * *

On our drive out of town, we pass the gas station and mini-mart at the corner of Joyce and Highway 101. The fuel price display, *120.9*, catches our attention.

"Went down," I say.

Prices are fluctuating a lot lately, but seldom in a downward direction.

"All over town," says John.

One nice thing about gas prices here – you don't have to shop around, since all stations change their prices in concert. It prevents gas wars and wasted bickering.

Farther down the road, we stop for our own fill-up. The price board says *123.9*.

"No way!" John almost yells in indignation.

"Let's go back," I suggest mockingly.

"Won't need to," he says. "We'll get them to bring their price down."

"Yeah, right."

We pull up to the main fuel aisle to fill up the truck first. Then we'll need to pull forward to pump the cheaper marine fuel, which is legal in our quads. A lanky teenage boy comes out of the office to pump our gas.

"You need to change your sign," says John. "It's down to one-twenty-point-nine in town."

"Really?" replies the boy.

I can tell he's just reacting to idle conversation, obviously lacking executive authority to change gas prices.

"I'll talk to Dick," says John, headed towards the office.

"This should go over good," I say to the kid.

The teenager nods, and his smile gives me the confidence in predicting we'll pay the full price.

When John returns, he announces: "Got it. Dick says he'll lower the price for us and change the sign. When we pull over to the other pump, I'll push for a lower price on marine gas."

* * * * *

Bro rides between John and me, plopped down and spread out in as many directions as he can. The cab is pretty full, with some of our riding gear and a few of John's tools packed at my feet. We exit Highway 101 at Dixon Road and leave the pavement approaching Lois Lake. At Tin Hat Junction, we leave the one-way portion of Goat Main, and John dials in the logging truck frequency on his VHF radio. One of the big controversies lately is the decision by logging companies to work on weekends. It's is purely economics, of course, enhanced by the anticipated summer fire danger that could shut down the forests to logging soon. Today, a Saturday, we could encounter logging trucks on these narrow mains. Quads would lose decisively in a head-to-head confrontation.

"Low-bed down nineteen," blares the radio.

A logging truck is pulling a large flatbed trailer, heading down the main from kilometre mark nineteen, a few klicks ahead.

"Shouldn't have to do this," says John. "Most people don't have a radio, so how are they going to know they're about to meet a speeding logging truck?"

Almost immediately, a black crew-cab pickup comes around the corner, headed towards us, slowing as it approaches. We mutually come to a stop, driver's door to driver's door, and John rolls down his window. The orange-vested driver of the "pilot car" speaks politely: "There's a low-bed behind me, about a kilometre. I'll tell him you're coming. There's a spot ahead where you can pull off to the side, just around the corner."

"Well, thanks for telling us," says John.

I know John well, and this is his sarcastic voice, but the vested driver takes it for a valid thank-you.

"You're welcome," he replies cheerily.

I swear it looks like steam pouring out of John's ears, but fortunately the black truck pulls away before John can comment further.

"You notice it's us whose supposed to pull off to the side," says John.

"Well, the low-bed is a lot bigger."

Just my contribution of fuel to add to the fire.

"Low-bed down seventeen," blares the radio.

We pull ahead past the curve, into the turnout at the side of the main. A few minutes later, the truck, hauling a large backhoe, rounds the corner ahead of us in a cloud of dust and blasts by. I wave. John doesn't.

* * * * *

Farther up the main, we turn off into a wide pullout area near Windsor Lake. Doug is waiting for us, ready to assist with our off-load. While I unstrap my quad, he hops aboard the trailer and climbs on my bike. Doug is like that – easy-going, quick to help, and immediately involved in anything that's happening. To jump onto someone else's

quad without asking permission is a rare action, but he does it with his normal easiness, so I immediately toss him the keys.

"Is this valet parking?" I ask.

"Sure. You can leave a small tip."

"Make it go," I say.

Doug starts my quad, and expertly backs it down the metal ramps. Then he helps John position his ramps from the tailgate of his Ford to the trailer. John drives down the first set of ramps, across the bed of the trailer, and down the rear ramps. Doug immediately pitches in to reload the ramps into John's truck. We leave the trailer connected to the truck, to speed loading when we return, ground-to-trailer, trailer-to-truck. Lazy but efficient.

As we gather our riding gear, Doug tells us about a bear he saw while waiting for us. He cruised back to Dodd Lake and saw the solo bear near the road. He describes the encounter with a low-key description, like he sees bears beside the road every day.

Today's ride is the beginning of the dusty summer season, so we'll need to keep a dust-length separation between us. That equates to

about a half-klick between quads. Doug leads for the first section of the ride (dustless), John and Bro ride in second position (dusty), and I bring up the rear (dustier).

We travel up Goat Lake Main (locally designated as Goat Main or Weldwood Main), past the junction with Rainbow Main, and beyond the entrance to the Goat 1 logging spur. When I pull into the wide parking area overlooking Goat Lake, John and Doug are talking with Jack, who they've come across in the middle of his solo ride. They're discussing the status of the landslides ahead and whether the creeks along D-Branch can be forded today. Our quad world is small, so there's no surprise at finding someone you know at a remote spot like this.

A few kilometres farther north, at the head of Goat Lake, a large flatbed barge and its tug are moored near a small dock built by Bob, a friend who sometimes brings his quad here by boat. The barge must have squeezed through Goat River that connects to Powell Lake. It seems inconceivable to move such a large barge through the narrow river, even at the current high-water level. And how could it be economical? To barge anything from here all the way back to Powell Lake's Block Bay seems illogical, since logging trucks could do the same job.

We come to the first landslide, and it's not stopping anyone. The fallen boulders and timber have been pushed away, and the remaining dirt is spread into a wide flat area. We need to go slow because of the sandy ruts and a few rocks, but the road is still open to most vehicles.

Farther up the Eldred River, the barge's purpose becomes evident, but the logic of such a means of transport seems even more questionable. At a wide turnout, we slow to weave our way through ten large pallets of shake-blocks spread across the road. The workers are finishing the packing, covering the wood blocks with heavy plastic.

A narrow winding path just big enough for quads has been cleared for recreational traffic like us. The workers have stopped to wait for us to pass through the maze. I wind through and wave at them, yelling "Hello!" They seem pleased to have the brief diversion of watching our small caravan.

It's likely the barge at the head of Goat Lake and these pallets are related. But the shake-blocks will need to be loaded on a truck, taken to the barge and reloaded there. Then the barge will need to wind back through Goat River, down Powell Lake to Block Bay. There the shakes will be off-loaded from the barge and reloaded on a truck. Wouldn't a single truck trip from here be more economical? It's often difficult to understand the logistics of log transport in the region, but there's no doubt the logging companies have worked it out to the nearest dollar.

We stop at the spot where we can view rock climbers scaling high granite cliffs on the other side of the Eldred River. It's so extreme that the climbers use a hanging line to repel themselves across the Eldred River to the base of the cliffs. The ascent is demanding, even for the most proficient rock climbers. Sometimes, they set up tents on the rock-wall to rest overnight during mid-climb. I doubt they sleep much, but their bedtime view must be spectacular. Today we don't see any climbers or their tents on the vertical wall.

Farther north, a few small trees have fallen across the road, but the obstacles are so minor we merely slow a bit and drive over them. In a few more klicks, the turnoff to the left (Dianne Main) leads across the Eldred River. We take the road leading to the right, now headed up the northernmost stretch of Goat Main. Finally, we leave the main where it intersects with D-Branch, which veers off to the east.

The going is easy at first. The dust is gone at these higher elevations, with wetter and less traveled trails. Without the dust, we can ride closer together. John stops, and I pull up behind him. He holds up four fingers, warning me the going ahead will require four-wheel drive. I hit the button that magically improves my traction, and we start upward on a narrow trail lying beside a nearly-dry, rocky creek.

The next landslide demands more skill to navigate. There are a few spots that could provide a problem for quad drivers, so we stop to make some trail improvements. Using a pry-bar and pick-ax, we clear

small boulders, clip bushes protruding into the trail, and fill some of the deepest ruts with small rocks and chunks of wood. John uses his chainsaw to trim up some of the scrub alders, and we're on our way again. I snap a few photos for John's next visit to the logging office.

By now, Mount Alfred is poking up at several viewpoints along the trail. It dominates the view to the east, although what we see for the next hour of riding isn't really the top of the mountain, although everyone refers to it as Mount Alfred. In reality, the 7800-foot summit is hidden behind the secondary triangular peak appearing in front of us. The crest we see is slightly lower than the very top of Mount Alfred, which is hidden just beyond.

Glaciers encircle the mountain, including an extensive ice-field to the left. Flying over Mount Alfred several years ago, John pointed to the huge glacier below us: "Doug has stood on top of that ice," he said. It was hard to believe – looking down from 10,000 feet – that anyone could climb to such a remote location. But knowing Doug, it's true. I'll use today's trip to ask him for the details of the climb.

The ride is challenging now, with several small creeks to cross, none of them beyond my limits. It's enjoyable knowing your limits,

and it's a skill that's taken quite a while to develop. Now I can sit at the edge of a stream or in the face of a rough stretch of trail and know whether it's within my capabilities. It's an important ability to develop, since knowing when it's safe to proceed is critical to riding on trails like these.

The cross-trenches are deep, slowing our progress even further. Branches and a few logs have fallen across portions of the trail, but all are small enough to drive over.

The third landslide needs work too, so we stop long enough to improve it for riders who may come after us. John's bad back seems a thing of the past.

In another kilometre, we come to the first major water obstacle. It's a roaring waterfall with a brief, flat level section between major cascades both above and below. Although it looks impressive, I'm confident this is within my capabilities. The waterfall above us is the most impressive part, but the drop-off below our flat crossing area is my biggest concern. Whitewater in the seemingly flat area obscures any large rocks jutting upward from the creek bottom. Such rocks could push a quad towards the waterfall downstream.

John calls it Spray Creek, with good reason, considering the nearness of the tumbling waterfall. But we don't stop long enough to take off our helmets and feel the spray. John crosses first, gets off his quad and comes back to point out the best route for Doug, who crosses next. Then it's my turn, and I cross without incident, although water splashes above my running boards. Exciting, but safe.

We pass through an area that required extensive clearing by John and his brother a few months ago. They groomed this narrow edge-of-ridge trail metre by metre, an arduous process. We crawl along this winding path called the "Bowling Alley," while huge boulders sit precariously perched above us on the edge of the cliff. The dramatic drop-off along the side and the rocks overhead are a bit unnerving, but it's more of a psychological hazard than a physical one. (The Bowling Alley is an appropriate name – the following spring, several 2-metre boulders fall to the trail below, temporarily closing it and requiring another strenuous session of trail clearing.)

Beyond the Bowling Alley, John lifts Bro from his aft-mounted box. The dog now walks behind his Grizzly. It's easier for Bro to walk

than ride in a rough spot like this, so I call Bro my trail roughness indicator. When Bro walks, expect tough going.

We cross another small creek, this one more scenic than difficult. Bro easily ambles through the water, behind John's quad. On the other side, a hockey stick is mounted on a fallen log above the bank. A sign on the log says: *Ice Lake Hockey Team – Next Game December 25; Tickets at Duck Lake.*

We pause below a rock-faced mountain, scanning for goats. John spots one right away, and walks back to my quad to help me find it. He describes the spot relative to a large landslide.

"Sorry, I can't see it," I admit.

"It's as clear as day."

By his tone, I can tell John is frustrated. He's loosing patience with me when it comes to looking for mountain goats. He turns and walks away without further comment, as if to punish me for my inferior eyesight compared to his keen visual acuity.

I watch John point out the goat's location to Doug, who spots the goat immediately. For me, it's necessary to pull binoculars from my

quad box. Then I see it clearly – an exceptionally large goat, grazing where there seems to be no vegetation. The animal stands motionless for several minutes while we wait for it to move again, but it doesn't. So I pack my binoculars away, and we continue up the trail.

At the next large creek, a new quad bridge sits beside an older footbridge. To prevent a washout, a double-deck culvert has been installed below the bridge. Today the creek barely flows through the top conduit, indicating a moderate water level. Culverts don't just pop up in remote locations like this. They have to be hauled in on quads, a demanding process.

These parallel bridges for hikers and quads are testament to an attempt to work together in enjoying the backcountry. It's not always an easy peace, but it's come a long ways in recent years. Much of the credit belongs to our local quad club president for conquering some of this fragile progress. Hikers shouldn't have to suffer the intrusion and commotion of passing quads on hiking trails. On the other hand, quad riders should have access to recreational areas where the environment can be properly protected. Hikers and bikers can get along together, but it takes compromises by both.

After passing the bridge, we enter a wide valley where cut alder branches lie across the trail. John and his brother, Rick, pruned this part of the trail two weeks ago, when it was covered with snow. Now we need to fine-tune the trail, removing the cut branches and using our garden clippers to remove additional overhanging boughs. John and I walk in front, clipping and removing some of the branches. Doug has the toughest job, coming along behind and dragging the remaining debris off the trail. Oh, did I mention John got his bad back last week by overdoing it while cutting a hedge in town?

"My friends in Los Angeles wouldn't believe this," I say. "I'll call them tomorrow and tell them I went on a wilderness ride on my quad. And that I spent most of the day picking up sticks on the trail to make it look pretty."

"It's not to make it look pretty," says John. "You know that."

"Yes, but it does seem like a bit of overkill."

"Don't forget the stick you picked up in your 'rad' last year."

He's right, a small stick was wedged in my radiator, resulting in an overheated engine, and it was a costly repair. Fortunately, I didn't break down in a remote area.

"Okay, you're right. But my friends in California will still think I'm crazy. It's really hard to describe this." I motion towards Mount Alfred, which looms straight ahead, huge glaciers spanning its sides.

"It's tremendous, isn't it?"

"It is, but not easy to describe."

I often try to tell my city-folk friends about the beauty of this region, but sometimes I think my attempts are futile, even with photos. I try to describe my floating cabin on Powell Lake, but the next time I see my California friends, they ask: "So how is your houseboat?" Well, it's not exactly a houseboat.

After nearly an hour of pruning the forest, we continue on. The farther we travel, the grander the waterfalls. In most places, you can look in any direction and see several large waterfalls plunging down the granite cliffs.

The end of the trail for quads is a large creek, roaring under a footbridge, with Mount Alfred looming in the background. It'll be another month before quads can ford this stream, and the end of summer before the new bridge is built. We take a break here and enjoy our lunch, while discussing how a bridge might be built at this spot.

Now here's a surprise (for me). We've been traveling almost constantly uphill today, but it's getting warmer as we climb. Snow patches sit by the side of the trail, but the air is distinctly warmer. John suggests we change from long-sleeves to short, as we prepare to climb farther. I pull my heavy shirt off, leaving my T-shirt.

"It shouldn't get warmer as we go up," I say.

"But we're getting farther inland as we climb," says John. "So it gets hotter."

"Sort of a tradeoff," I surmise. "You go higher and it gets cooler, but you go farther from the ocean and it gets warmer. The diminished cooling power of the ocean outweighs the cooling affect of altitude."

"Good day for hiking," says John. "And the snow patches keep the bugs away. But the snow up high is melting fast."

I never thought of that either. There's an important hint here regarding our return trip that I should notice, but I ignore it.

"It's too far to make it to Ice Lake today?" I ask.

I know the answer, but still there's hope.

"Long way for this time of day," says John. "Besides, the trail will need some major clipping to get through on the first hike of the season."

I'd just as soon be done with pruning shears for the day. So I'll be content with an alternate hike.

"We can make it to Big Tree, easy," says John. "Bring your clippers."

I guess I better not put away my pruning shears quite yet.

We walk across the narrow wooden bridge, and clip our way along the trail, once again cutting the scrub alders at the sides, John on the left and me on the right, while Bro supervises and sniffs for bears. That again leaves Doug with the unglamorous job of picking up the branches. As always, he does the task without a single complaint. In fact, he's so thorough that we get far ahead of him. But we know he's back there, working away the entire time.

When the Ice Lake trail splits off, I almost don't see the intersection. In fact, if John hadn't pointed it out, I wouldn't have noticed it at all – it's that overgrown. Getting through to the lake in a few weeks, one of John's goals, will be a major challenge. Added to the obstacles of the path's tangle of alders is the steep uphill climb.

We continue along the trail to Big Tree, which becomes more open (less pruning!) the farther we go. Finally, it's all rock, an old landslide of sharp-edged boulders mixed with a few logs. We climb upward to Big Tree, one of the biggest fir trees in the region, three metres in diameter. Old Gnarly, near Okeover Inlet, is supposedly the biggest fir in the immediate vicinity of Powell River, but I've stood near Gnarly, and this tree seems significantly larger. In a few minutes, Doug joins us, and I snap his picture in front of the tree. But a smaller (not small) cedar in front of Big Tree obscures some of its trunk.

This giant tree is part of an extensive grove of old-growth left behind by loggers for unexplained reasons. I'd like to believe they left these firs for us to enjoy.

We hike a bit farther, crossing a small creek, and step out into a meadow where we have a direct view of Mount Alfred and Doug's glacier on its left. I ask Doug about the difficulty of the climb, and he

describes it as "a horrible hike, but beautiful at the same time." That's not hard to understand.

When we return to Big Tree and are ready to start back to our quads, Doug notices a waterfall well above us, nearly hidden between the trees. Maybe we can get to it by walking along the creek.

We climb higher. The creek splits, and both branches get wider. We hop cross the rivulets several times, trying to stay out of the dense brush. At some crossing spots, the creek it fairly wide, and I get my boots wet. I feel water seeping into my socks. My feet are a bit cold now, and it's a sloggy feeling as I walk, but it's a warm day. I can wait to change my socks when I'm back at my quad.

Soon we are in the midst of thorny devil's club, best to be avoided at all cost. It doesn't look any better higher up, so we give up and descend back down to Big Tree. Then we hike back out the trail, headed for our quads.

I walk in front of Doug and John, wanting to get back first so I can fish near the footbridge for a few minutes without holding everybody up. I keep a fast pace and soon am well ahead of the other three hikers (don't forget Bro!).

Back at my quad, I pull a spare set of socks from my backpack, and treat myself to dry, warm feet. If I could carry only one item of spare clothing when on the trail, it would definitely be socks.

The water below the footbridge is so swift I can't keep my collapsible fishing pole's lure in the water. The red-and-white daredevil repeatedly bounces off the top of the swirling whitewater and eventually hooks on a snag at the edge of the creek. I get my favourite lure back by crawling down the bank. It's obvious I'm not going to be able to catch a fish here.

Since John and Doug aren't back yet, I hike downstream to a spot that's a bit more open. Still, the water is tumbling too fast. It's impossible to keep my lure in the water, except in spots running so fast no reasonable trout would enter. It's likely this glacier-fed creek is sterile anyway. But, as always, I enjoy the experience of fishing, just for the sake of trying.

It's now obvious – John and Doug haven't hiked directly back to the quads, or they'd be here by now. Where could they have gone? They'd better not be on their way to Ice Lake without me!

While waiting, I make four snowballs from the crystalline snow near our quads. Then I sit on the logs near the footbridge, snowballs hidden beside me, and wait. When John and Doug start across the bridge, I'll catch them by surprise.

In just a few more minutes, I see Bro approaching the bridge. John can't be far behind. Sure enough, John comes out into the clearing.

"You better not have gone to Ice Lake without me!" I yell.

"We sure did," taunts John.

"No way!" I shout, as he starts across the bridge. Just then, Doug pops out of the clearing behind him.

I let loose with the first snowball: "Bombs away!" I yell.

It catches John by surprise, but the snowball sails well off to the side, and he retreats back to the other side of the bridge. I watch Doug and John consult briefly. Then John starts across the bridge again, and I let loose with another shot. I miss again, but quickly reload with another snowball. This time I'm on my mark, but John catches it in mid-air and throws the fragmented remains back at me. Then he retreats again.

"Okay, we didn't go to Ice Lake," says John. "We just clipped the first part of the trail.

"Too late. You're in my gun sights."

Doug tries to cross next. I wait until he gets to mid-bridge before I let loose with my final snowball. He ducks, and the last of my ammunition sails over his head. Four bombs – no strikes.

This should be the end of the story, since all that remains is the ride home. Typically, the homeward segment isn't nearly as interesting as the trip to your destination. That's only natural, since you're usually retracing your path. The exception is when you're able to select a loop for a trip, returning by a different route. But that's difficult in this region, so usually you ride straight back, with few stops to prompt excitement. Of course, there are variables in such a scenario. Even changes in weather and sun angle can make a big difference in how you see things. And there are side trails and mechanical problems to wreak variety (and havoc). But all-and-all, the trip to your destination holds most of your interest.

As we leave the footbridge at the last major creek on the trail to Ice Lake, all seems routine. The day is warm and sunny, with plenty of daylight remaining. Our quads are running fine, and the trip is all but over. But warm and sunny is the rub. Which requires a whole new chapter.

Chapter 3

Boys' Night Out

Warm and sunny. We start back down the trail from (almost) Ice Lake with plenty of energy. It's a perfect day for riding. Although we haven't made it all the way to the lake, seeing Mount Alfred up close and personal has rewarded us.

We pass the spot where we stopped and watched the mountain goat earlier in the day. We barely slow down, but I glance upward long enough to notice the small white dot missing from the area below the landslide where it stood for so long.

We pause briefly at the wooden bridge with the dual culverts, refilling our water bottles in the clear stream. The cold water tastes amazingly refreshing, and I drink nearly a full bottle. The water is now gushing higher through the upper culvert than a few hours ago, or so it seems. It's just one of those things resulting from a temporary change in stream conditions, caused by any number of factors, such as a break in a log jam. Or it might just be my imagination. I'm sure John notices it too (he misses nothing), but he doesn't say anything, nor do I.

We ford several small creeks. When we arrive at a larger stream, I'm disoriented. I remember crossing at the waterfall below Spray Creek as the biggest challenge on the way in, but this is a different spot. From my recollection, the boulders are all out of place from anywhere we've been today. This creek is big and running white, but I don't even remember it from the ride in. It looks somewhat like Spray Creek, but not quite the same. We cross without incident.

When riding with John, I seldom pay close attention to our route. It's a lot like riding as a passenger in a car. Why contemplate navigation when someone else is driving? I admit to myself that this creek crossing seems unfamiliar, as if it's a completely different stream. But we are on the same trail – of that I'm certain.

We enter the rough area where John let Bro walk on the way in, and once again the dog trots behind John's quad. However, from my position behind John, the black Lab seems to be working harder now, probably tired from what has already been a long day on the trail. And the trail appears more rutted, muddier too. Of course, we were through here only a few hours ago, which might explain the ruts, but why is it wetter? In front of me, water trickles from the edges of the trail, down into the center of John's muddy tire tracks. I watch Bro splash behind the quad, panting and trying to keep pace.

We pass along the precipitous Bowling Alley, less adrenalin-producing than the first time through. In another kilometre, John slows, turns in his seat, and points ahead to a giant waterfall, one of the biggest we've seen all day. Traveling in the opposite direction on the way in, this waterfall was behind us and unnoticed. Could this be the tumbling water above Spray Creek? If so, it's formidable looking from this angle. I turn to look behind me, where Doug now rides. He waves and nods his head in acknowledgement of the plunging cascades.

With the waterfall looming ever bigger as we approach, I'm again confused. (Could it have been my drink of "tainted" water at the bridge?) We are headed directly towards the falls, so it seems we'll have to cross it, but we've already forded Spray Creek, the major obstacle behind us. Or have we?

We angle down a gently sloping hill, the trail widens, and a violent river stands right in front of us. Water tumbles through rapids that seem too big to cross. To our right (and uphill) is a huge waterfall, dangerously close to our crossing spot. To the left (downstream) is a steep drop-off, much too close to the path we'll need to follow through the river. Mist from the tumbling water sprays up all around. Now I get it – sort of. This is Spray Creek, but the water is much more violent now. And the roaring creek a kilometre back was the small, easily-crossed stream we encountered on our ride earlier today. But how could everything have changed so fast?

We get off our quads and walk back along the trail to get away from the spray and noise of the waterfall. John is the first to speak, and he directs it to me.

"I was afraid of this," he says. "Doug and I talked about it, but I thought it would be okay. We knew the creeks would grow today?"

"Why?"

I'm the amateur scientist among us, but the physics of this has gotten away from me. I know creeks subside gradually over the summer, so why are these streams growing into major rivers on such a pleasant day? Oh! – it hits me – because it's warm and sunny. Simultaneously, John answers me.

"Because the snow is melting like mad today," he says. "Based on what we saw when we came in earlier, I thought we would be okay. But I was wrong."

John was wrong. I've never heard him say such a thing before. I never think of John as being wrong. I'm not sure I believe it.

"Man, that thing is really roaring," I say.

I'm sure my eyes are as big as saucers.

"It should be safe to cross," says John. "Let's go back and take a closer look."

It doesn't look safe to me. John admits it looks only marginally okay to him, but he points out the recommended route across. It's

pretty much the same path as before, but more rocks are submerged and impossible to see. I don't like it, and neither does Doug.

"We'll have to stay way clear of the drop-off downstream," says Doug. "The current could push you over the edge, if you aren't careful."

"I'm sure it's crossable," says John. "Watch where I go, and you can modify your path from what you learn by watching me. After I get across, I'll park, and we can talk about it."

"Okay," says Doug, sounding confident.

"Okay," I say, far less confident.

John picks up Bro and hoists him into his box. The dog won't be able to walk across this creek, and John can use the added weight. His bike is bigger and heavier than ours, but every pound counts.

After pausing just a moment to finalize the path in his mind, John shifts into four-wheel drive and advances the Grizzly's thumb-throttle. At first, he drives slowly, but by midstream we can see the water come over his running boards, and his bike starts to drift towards the drop-off. The quad is a victim of the powerful current, so John guns it, fishtails a bit, and plunges the final few metres to the other side as water splashes everywhere. He's safe on shore in just a few seconds, but he's soaking wet from the waist down.

John drives up the rocky bank and parks, partly out of sight behind some bushes. Then he walks back down to talk to us. Bro follows behind, splashing into the water to play.

But none of us can talk. We all have to holler to be heard over the roaring water. Even then, it takes repeated shouts to get our messages across.

"I don't like it!" yells Doug. "You almost lost it!"

"It felt okay!" hollers John. "But aim a little farther to the right than I did, to counter the current."

"Our bikes are lighter!" shouts Doug. "I'm not in a hurry! I think I'll stay right here tonight!"

"What?" yells John.

I'm sure he heard Doug perfectly, but he'd prefer not to admit it. As for me, I'm relieved that Doug is thinking this through. My mind races, pondering how we can weigh our bikes down for increased stability in the creek, but our quad racks are already nearly filled. I didn't like what I saw when John crossed, and I'd be glad to stay here tonight, waiting as long as necessary for the water to recede. But if the snow continues to melt, won't the stream continue to rise even more? Maybe waiting "long enough" means all summer or an expensive helicopter ride back home.

Our shouted messages go on for about ten minutes, many of our attempts at communications requiring repeated yells. Finally, our "conversation" is interrupted when John holds up his palm ("Wait!") and runs back up to his quad. It's a purposeful trot. When he comes back down the hill, he's carrying a heavy rope.

"Probably not long enough!" he shouts. "Catch!"

His toss is perfect, but the end of the rope falls short by about a metre. John draws the rope back across the water and trots up the hill again. This time he drives back down in his quad. He positions his Grizz facing us in the shallow water on his side of the river, ties the rope to the hook of his winch, and begins extending the metal cable. When it's long enough, he tosses the extended rope again. Doug catches it and pulls it up the shore. John plays out some more cable from his winch, and Doug attaches the end-loop of the rope around the handlebar of his quad.

"Let's think about this," says Doug. "I don't like the idea of being winched across."

"John can't retract the winch very fast, so you'd have to go slow," I say with concern.

"And if you outrun the cable, it could get hung up under the quad," says Doug.

"When I go across, I want to go fast," I add. "I don't want to be worrying about the winch cable getting tangled under my bike."

We sit at the edge of the whitewater on our respective sides of the creek for several minutes, nobody saying anything – just thinking to ourselves as we ponder the cable and it's attached rope. None of us come up with any solutions. Instead, we manage to get soaked, just standing around. Spray Creek deserves its name – a continual heavy mist surges down onto us from the falls above. The spray is light but persistent, punctuated by a soaking blast when the breeze shifts slightly.

John shrugs his shoulders and yells something. We don't understand a word of it. Then he walks back up the hill, and veers off to the left, out of sight.

"Where's he going?" I ask.

"Don't know," says Doug, ever easy-going. "Maybe he needs to take a leak. The crossing scared the piss out of him."

Then we see the smoke from a fire John has started.

"He starting a fire," I say. "What do you think that means?"

"I'm not sure," replies Doug. "Maybe he plans to stay over there tonight. Or maybe he's sending smoke signals for help."

Pretty soon, we're laughing like mad. Here we are: on the wrong side of a raging creek we're afraid to cross, about to spend the night with no camping gear, and no guarantee the creek will be better rather than worse in the morning. But it's pretty funny. John's unexplained fire simply adds to the implausible situation.

While John is playing with his fire, Doug and I come to an easy decision.

"We could probably make it without a problem," he says. "But getting back to town isn't that important."

"Better safe than sorry." I cringe as I say it – What a cliché, but true.

When John comes back down the trail to the creek, I holler the most pressing question we have.

"Why the fire?"

"I got cold!" hollers John. "Got wet from the crossing, and there's more spray from the waterfall on this side."

"Oh, okay. We're staying!"

"What?" yells John.

I raise my hand in a good-bye wave, and then tuck my hand in close to my chest as I wave again like a child.

John shakes his head: *No!*

I wave bye-bye again, offering a broad, artificial smile that definitely shows my teeth. Then I put my palms together and lay my head to the side in a now-I-lay-me-down motion.

He shakes his head again, so I go through the good-bye and sleep motions again. Then I yell as loud as I can, speaking very slowly and pausing between every word.

"Look! – We need you back at town, not here!" I shout. "You need to call our wives and let them know we're fine. And your family will be worried if you don't come home. So go home!"

It takes a lot of loud effort to get my message across, but it's because he refuses to listen.

"Go home!" yells Doug.

"Okay, I'll go!" he finally replies. "But wait a minute."

He runs back up the hill.

I know how hard this is for John. He refuses to leave anyone behind anywhere, anytime. It's often more efficient for John and I to ride ahead of Margy on tough stretches of trail, particularly if we're returning in a short while, and Margy feels comfortable with this. But John always hates to leave her behind. Just like the Marine Corps - leave no man (or woman) behind!

When John returns to the shore, he holds up a plastic bag and tosses it to our side of the creek. Doug catches it in mid-air, a perfect shot.

"Ouch!" says Doug.

The bag has a rock inside for weight. And a bunch of smashed stuff – cookies, potato chips, and three miniature candy bars.

"Thanks!" Doug shouts back across the creek.

"Hey, wrap my jacket around a rock, and throw it over!" hollers John.

I've been carrying John's jacket on my quad all day, a common occurrence when he runs out of room with Bro in the aft box and a chainsaw in front. This is the perfect heavy clothing for tonight – an inner lining with a separate outer jacket, and rainproof – a two-for-one coat that should be enough to keep Doug and me warm.

"No way!" I shout back. "We're about to spend the night in the woods, and you want your jacket back?"

"I'm cold!" he says. He makes a shivering motion with his arms wrapped around his chest.

"Be cold!" shouts Doug. "You'll be home before sunset!"

"Do you have matches?" yells John.

"I've got a lighter!" I shout.

It's just now that I remember the cheap fluid-filled lighter Margy insists I carry in my backpack. She bought three – one for John, too

– 19 cents each at Liquidation World. I almost threw mine away, but then decided to put it in my pack. It's been sitting there, unused, for months. Thank you, Margy!

"Anything else you can think of?" asks John.

"Beer!" I shout. "Now go!"

"I'm gone!"

It's probably one of the hardest things John has ever had to do.

Doug unhooks the rope from his quad: "Let's keep the rope," he says to me. "Might need it."

I unhook the rope from the cable, and John retracts his winch. The cable's hook gets hung up on a rock on John's side of the creek.

"That would be a bad thing," I say to Doug.

We watch John yank on the cable a few times, and finally it breaks loose.

Doug and I stand on the shore of the creek in the late afternoon light, watching John lift Bro into his quad box. Then he climbs on his Grizz. Over the roar of the water, we can't hear him start his engine, but we watch him slowly pull away, stopping briefly to douse his fire. Then he drives back to the bank, pauses briefly and waves. We wave back, and he drives away, out of sight into the trees.

"Why don't we stay on this side tonight?" I say to Doug, as if there's still a choice.

"At least we agree about something."

It's a good start.

* * * * *

Doug and I drive our quads slowly back up the trail. There's no hurry – we've got time to kill. We pass a wide turnout, drive for another half-klick, then turn around and return to the turnout.

"Looks good to me," I say.

"Maybe too exposed. We could camp in the woods."

"I'd feel more comfortable here," I admit. "Bugs should be less too."

"It's fine with me."

Everything is always fine with Doug.

Our first priority is to gather firewood, which is a fairly easy task. Small branches, dry and ready to burn, are everywhere. We also find a few chunks of broken logs. Soon we have a large pile of wood. Doug piles some rocks in a circle to form a fire-ring.

When we're finished, I take a few minutes to pull everything out of my backpack, looking for useful items. John always accuses me of traveling too heavy, but today I'm glad to have a full pack. I find some good stuff, including a flashlight, mosquito repellant, a compact rain jacket, a chart of the constellations, some small hand tools, a bag of peanuts, an electronic compass, milk bones for Bro (I hope I won't have to turn to these!), and my miniature electronic voice recorder.

"Hey, I've found a neat source of entertainment," I tell Doug.

"A radio?" asks Doug.

"No, a tape recorder."

"Doesn't sound like fun to me," replies Doug.

Maybe he knows what I have in mind.

Doug's supplies include valuable caches of food: chocolate bars, crispy potato chips, and an apple. He even has two small slices of watermelon, which we immediately attack. Best watermelon I've ever tasted.

What we don't have is sleeping gear. We didn't come prepared for an overnight stay. There's only so much room on a quad. You can carry sleeping bags and tents, but there wouldn't be room for much else. Today we've carried equipment for day-use comfort only.

Doug uses his pick-ax (conveniently strapped to the front of his quad for trail building) to clear rocks from the area we select for our beds. We spend a lot of time preparing our campsite, partly because it's important, and partly because we have nothing else to do. Days are long in early June, and it's still a long time to darkness.

We work together to prepare small cedar boughs as a mattress. I tug on the lower limbs, drawing them close enough to the ground so Doug can clip them with my pruning shears (a multipurpose trail clearing tool).

In the area where we're gathering the cedar, we find bear scat, and there's more along the road. Doug and I don't talk about it, but we're both thinking the same thing, I'm sure. We'll keep the fire going all

night, and both of us have a knife handy – Doug's is significantly heftier than mine.

We drag the branches back to our campsite and cut off thin boughs, spreading them into two piles. We spend a lot of time with this – it'll be nice to have soft beds, plus we have a lot of time to kill.

It's amazing how soft a pile of boughs can be. Cedars are the tree-of-choice for this important task, beating out the less-awesome fir. Over the years, I've become a cedar lover, and my preference for the species is confirmed again tonight.

Once our camp is set up, we drive back down to Spray Creek to see if there has been any change. If anything, the water is roaring even faster now. To the east, the high peaks are catching the light of sunset – snow is still melting and feeding the streams in the high country. Before heading back up the road, I take a photo of Spray Creek, looking up the waterfall from our only possible crossing spot.

When we arrive back at the campsite, we position our quads on the uphill side of our cedar beds, to block tonight's expected downslope

wind. Then we start the fire, a tentative flame at first. Within a few minutes, we have a stable blaze we'll tend the entire night.

After sunset, while I mind the fire, Doug drives back down the hill to the creek again. When he leaves, he switches on his headlights, and they provide a bright, cheery message proclaiming we're in charge of ourselves. It may not be very dark yet, and there's no one around for kilometres, but Doug can still turn on his headlights for oncoming traffic, if he wants to. Neither Doug nor I have ever driven our quads at night. I routinely run with my lights on during the daylight on logging roads, as a safety measure, but neither of us has used our headlights after dark. When Doug returns from the creek, it's reassuring to see his bright lights coming up the hill. He reports there is no change in the creek's flow.

I've been considering the situation. What if the flow gets worse? Staying here more than one night with our limited snacks would be challenging. And rain is in the forecast after tomorrow. More water will raise the creek level even more, to say nothing of making a mess

out of sleeping in the open without a tent or even a tarp. These are things best not pondered tonight. What we need now is a diversion from our concerns, so it's time to turn to high-tech entertainment.

"It's time for the interview," I say as I sit down on a rock-and-board bench Doug has built near the fire.

"I'm not sure I'm ready for this," says Doug.

"Just talk into the microphone. It'll be easy."

Doug sits next to me on the makeshift bench, and I position the miniature voice recorder between us. It's easy for me, and seems so for Doug. In fact, he has lots to say.

* * * * *

Doug came to Canada from New Zealand in 1983, working his first winter in a fabrication shop at 100 Mile House, and then in construction of a sawmill. He moved to Tumbler Ridge in 1984, where he lived in a brand new town created near a coal mine. There he was employed as a millwright (industrial mechanic) until 1988. Then Doug moved to Powell River to work in the paper mill, the same mill where his grandfather was a member of the construction crew in the 1930s. He calls it a "big circle in life."

Comparing Powell River to New Zealand, he sees similarities in the outdoors (the "bush"), and the ocean. An avid outdoorsman, Doug climbed all the way to the top of Mount Alfred with four friends a decade ago. Their route began as ours did today, traveling by truck up D-Branch a short ways. They left their two vehicles and started up a series of switchbacks that are now overgrown and impassable. They then followed a logging slash: "Nearly straight up to an old trail originally blazed by a fellow named Higgins years ago. Horrible but beautiful at the same time. The trail led to a beautiful meadow and a ridge above, where we camped the first night."

On the second day, they tried to hike farther, but fog enshrouded the ridge, driving them back to their original campsite, where they were forced to remain all day.

"The following morning we arose at 4:30, kept the campsite set up, and left with only daypacks to try hiking to Mount Alfred. We followed the ridge out to a mountain called Ironside at the base of the glacier. There was no real trail – it's all open on the ridge, so you just see the glacier and head for it. From Ironside, we followed a dry waterfall all the way up to the glacier on Mount Alfred."

On the ice sheet, they strapped metal-spiked crampons onto their boots for added grip, tied themselves together with a rope, and started across the glacier, using ice axes to assist. They finally reached the snow-face near the peak of Mount Alfred, and then made their final 1500-foot ascent to the top.

"On the glacier, there were lots of crevasses, some about four-feet across, and we had to jump over. But when we reached the top of Alfred, it was fairly flat, lots of room. We could look back towards Queens Reach and Princess Louisa Inlet. Best view I've ever seen."

Doug and his friends hiked back to their ridgeline base camp the same day. They stayed overnight again, and then hiked back down to their trucks.

Doug has seen Mount Alfred up-close from the other side too, when he and John boated to the head of Jervis Inlet, and rode motorcycles up the valley (*Up the Strait*, Chapter 5).

"We rode to a spot about 3 kilometres from Ice Lake on the other side. It's not as steep as this side, so it would be possible to build switchbacks and hike down to Jervis Inlet from Ice Lake. The trees are spaced quite a ways apart. Fairly steep, but it's probably achievable."

Doug wants to climb Mount Alfred again, and he has a planned route: "Maybe try it from the Big Tree side, where we were today. There's a tagged trail all the way up."

My prediction – Doug will be on top of Mount Alfred again soon.

* * * * *

After the recorded interview, we rest on our reasonably-soft cedar boughs, fighting off the bugs (less than expected) by making sure our entire bodies are covered with clothing. Our hands and wrists are covered with heavy gloves, shirt sleeves tucked inside. Our pants legs are pushed into our boots, and I wear my full-face ski mask. If necessary, we could sleep in our helmets.

My cedar bed is comfortable, using my helmet bag as a pillow, stuffed with extra gloves and other soft materials I've found. But neither of us gets much sleep. When the fire dies low, we alternately get up to tend it. It's important to keep it going, but I worry about too large a fire, considering the risk posed by sparks in the forest.

The Big Dipper drops low in the north, and I remind Doug how to use the pointer stars to find Polaris. I also give him an eye test (which he passes), using the double stars in the Dipper's handle, Mizar and Alcor. During the night, twice when I awake from fitful sleep, I watch the International Space Station pass overhead. There's no doubt this is what I'm watching, since I've seen the Station many times. But it's somewhat rare to catch a view of its passage on an unscheduled basis. Usually you need to know when and where to look. Tonight I'm treated to two passes without any preparation, an indicator all is well in the world and high above it, too.

The temperature is cool, but not extremely cold, dropping to about 5 degrees C. I'm glad to be wearing John's inner jacket over my T-shirt, covered by a long-sleeved shirt, and rain jacket. Doug wears John's outer jacket over his lighter clothing. I resolve to never let John forget how resistant he was to leaving without his jacket – the poor baby is sleeping comfortably in his bed in town tonight!

As I doze without sound sleep, my thoughts wander to bears, although I feel confident we've selected a good campsite, and the fire should ward off any big animals. My greater concern is what we'll find at Spray Creek in the morning. Tonight, the sound of waterfalls surround us in all directions – some big roars, along with smaller echoes, but all contribute to the background drone of tumbling water. Sometimes the rumble seems to lessen; then it seems louder, changing with the direction of the night's downslope wind. I lie awake, worried more about the level of creeks than being attacked by a bear.

At 3 am, I get up to stoke the fire. To the north, dim twilight radiates above the mountain-shrouded horizon. During June, a hint of sunlight lasts all night at this latitude. The sun sinks in the northwest, but rides only slightly below the horizon, until it rises again in the northeast. It's dark for several hours, but the dim glow is visible all night.

We're up and ready to go shortly after 5 am. By now, there's plenty of light to see the road, so we douse our campfire, pack up, and drive down to the creek. We drive slowly, not sure we want to see the results of the cooler morning temperatures. Has it been enough to bring the water level down, especially considering how long it must take for yesterday's snow melt to make it down the slopes?

Pleasant surprise! The flow is less. We can see rocks near our side of the creek that weren't visible during our near-sunset visit. And the rapids near the center of the creek are obviously tamer now. We can make it across with little worry.

Doug goes first (after all, he's more experienced), and I notice he slides a bit downstream in the rapids, but he makes it through fine. I follow his path, gunning it at midstream to assure I don't drift precariously towards the drop-off. Then – I'm safe on the other side!

From here it's a pleasant early morning ride back to Doug's truck, where John has left my quad trailer. We're home by 9 am – boys' night out. We'll both sleep well tonight, and we won't even need to wear John's jacket.

Chapter 4

Theodosia

I'm sure it aggravates avid motorcycle riders when quad owners refer to their machines as "bikes." But it's an appropriate description for quads. In fact, earlier all-terrain vehicles predating the quad craze were bikes in an even truer sense of the word: they were three-wheel designs that could be described as powered tricycles. Their instability and accident-prone history led to a lot of bad press, but ATVs quickly evolved through this early stage to the quad of present day. For today's rider of even the biggest quad, it's still a bike.

Margy's first quad was a small two-wheel drive Honda that served her well. The lack of four-wheel drive, although a limitation, seldom kept her from going anywhere we went together. Even in snow, she would bog down only a few metres before my bigger Kodiak. And the smaller dimensions of Margy's bike were comfortable for her 5-foot 1-inch frame. The advantage of maneuverability outweighed the few times when two-wheel drive was a limitation.

But over time, Margy longed for the comfort of four-wheel drive. In her case, the reassurance of this added feature equated to a sense of confidence in the trail ahead. The heavier weight of a bigger bike, coupled with more traction, would allow a much more stable climb up those steep hills. Rather than making a running start and leaning ahead to keep the front of her quad grounded, she could climb slowly up the same slope in four-wheel drive. The maneuverability of newer quads, even bigger models, has improved in recent years to the point where they equal Margy's original, smaller bike.

She (correction: John) sold her bike when she (and John) decided she should buy a Kodiak 450. It'll be a stock quad, except for the colour. For a few extra dollars, Margy decided to order a silver one, and it seemed worth waiting for a bike not currently in local supply.

The dealer quickly locates a silver Kodiak in Alberta, and it should be here in two weeks. But over a month goes by, with no specific date for delivery. I've been through this before. Powell River may be only a little over a 100 klicks north of Vancouver, but it takes a barge (or two-ferries) to get a big piece of equipment to the consumer. Once, when waiting for delivery of an outboard motor, I experienced two months of agonizing delay. Since then, I've learned – getting a quad from Alberta won't be a fast process.

When a special incentive offer for the purchase of the Kodiak begins to run out, I call to check. I'm assured the promise of a free winch will still be honoured after the first of the month.

"I'll check on a delivery date again," says Danny. "But when you order something from back east, that's what you can expect."

So Alberta is "back east." Anything the other side of Vancouver is far enough away to make Powell River a remote delivery destination.

Finally, the silver quad arrives, and John takes delivery while Margy and I are in the States. He installs an aft carrying case, mirror, and takes a short test drive around the block. After losing half of the summer awaiting delivery, Margy is finally ready to ride.

The first day back at our cabin, Margy sprains her ankle while walking across the bridge to shore. She misses the first step and tumbles to the walkway, while I watch helplessly from the front porch. She falls forward on the wooden bridge. *Crack!*

We both hear it, and our first thought is a broken bone, but the *Crack!* is merely an overstressed cedar board that takes the brunt of her fall. Still, it's a bad sprain.

Margy has been the victim of numerous twisted ankles over the years, always with a prolonged recovery period. We both know this will be no different. There'll be no quad riding for at least another month.

* * * * *

The silver quad sits on our trailer at the airport, awaiting its first ride. The old trailer tires aren't right for this heavier load, so John installs new ones. Now that we have two Kodiak 450s on a single-axle carrier, the U-built will be put to the test. Considering the trailer's recent history (a broken leaf spring), the safe transport of our quads into the backcountry is somewhat questionable.

By mid-August, Margy's ankle is adequately healed for a quad trip, and we plan to depart on the first good-weather day. John is balancing his schedule between a solo trip up D-Branch towards Mount Alfred and a ride accompanying us on the break-in voyage. I'd prefer to have him along for our first ride, but a Mount Alfred trip is too long – we don't want to risk being stranded far from home if there are problems with the new bike.

John's considers his Mount Alfred trip a priority, but it demands nearly perfect weather conditions. This time of year, the slightest weather disturbance in Powell River can equate to drenching rain in the high country. If the weather is perfect, it's Mount Alfred. If it's marginal, he'll join us for the break-in ride.

From our cabin, I telephone John at 8:00 am to determine the weather decision. The conditions, at least as viewed from Hole in the Wall, are far from perfect.

"No Mount Alfred today," announces John. "But it looks good enough for Theo."

"We'll get started right way," I reply. "But it'll take awhile to get down the lake and hook up the trailer."

It's an excuse. I'm always running late for John's fast-paced schedule. The trailer hook-up is complicated by the storage of our quads at the airport. But the hangar is a good spot for our large equipment. Living in a floating cabin has its drawbacks. We're forever pressed for storage space.

Our ride down the lake is quick, but I can't get by without breakfast before a ride, so we take time to stop at the drive-through for a McMuffin to eat on the way to the airport. By the time we pull up to the hangar, we're barely within the schedule we've promised to John.

The hook-up goes fine, but we run into Bob (who is working on his airplane), and then Wally and Don at the Flying Club. It'll slow us down to stop and talk, but I can't pass up the opportunity. The airport is a source of endless interaction, and I love it. But I don't like the latest report on Selina's engine – her airplane has a Franklin with a busted crankshaft. Try to get one of those rare motors delivered to Powell River by barge or truck.

As Margy drives us down Duncan Avenue from the airport, with our trailer in tow, I glance at my watch. It's already well past 10 o'clock, our appointed time to meet John. He isn't going to like this.

"Drop me off at the corner by John's house," I instruct Margy. "You can continue down to the alley, and then head back to his driveway. It'll leave you parked in the right direction at John's house."

The routes to the bush are limited. Since we'll need to top off our bikes with gas, it's either north or south on Joyce Avenue to a gas station. Today it'll definitely be north, since we're headed to Theodosia. By driving around the block, Margy will be pointed in the right direction. Swinging the trailer around at John's house isn't her favourite sport. In the meantime, I'll get to John's a few minutes before her.

Of course, I know John is already wondering why we're late. So I hop out of the truck at the corner, trot down the street, and John meets me as I enter the yard.

"Hey, where did you come from?" he asks.

"Oh, things were getting behind schedule, so I left Margy at the airport and walked down from there."

"Oh," he replies.

Just an "Oh." Does John really think I walked all that way? But he doesn't question the logic, grabs his lunch and backpack, and ushers Bro to his truck. His quad is already loaded in the back of his pickup, and he's ready to roll. I expected criticism for being late (again), but instead it's just an "Oh."

As John helps Bro into his truck with an ass-push, Margy appears in the alley. She pulls up perpendicular to the driveway, headed in the right direction and ready to go.

"Hey, there's Margy now," says John.

I'm almost certain he knows we drove from the airport together, but he won't give me a break by admitting it. With John, you can never win.

* * * * *

We pull into the gas station in our normal order. John uses one side of the dual regular-marine gas pump, and we take the other. We pump regular fuel into our trucks, marine gas into the three quads. It's an efficient process that leaves us ready to pull out onto Joyce Avenue, headed in the right direction. But our progress is slowed when Arnie pulls into the next lane at the pumps.

"Where you goin'?" asks Arnie.

He doesn't need gas, but saw John parked at the pumps and stopped to investigate.

"Theo," replies John. "Want to come?"

When we're at the gas station, it's a rare stop without seeing someone John knows.

"Actually, I've got the day off," says Arnie. "Maybe I'll join you later. Where do you plan to park?"

There are only so many preferred parking spots on this route, and Arnie is familiar with ours. He's obviously a rider John knows well, although I don't recognize him. Then again, when I meet people on the trail, everyone looks the same in their helmets. Local tradition is to stop and talk, but never ask for names, hoping you'll recognize identities through their helmets before your conversation is over. Others accomplish this well, but I seldom figure out with whom I'm talking.

Arnie drives away, and Jim pulls into his vacated spot. In the bed of Jim's pickup is his Grizzly. As he begins to pump his gas, I approach his truck. Maybe John has already invited him to go along.

"Joining us?" I ask.

"Guess so," Jim replies. "Going to Theo?"

Undoubtedly, John has already told him about our plans. It's a small town. And this three-person (and a dog) ride is getting bigger by the minute.

"Theo it is," I say. "Do you know where we plan to off-load?"

"Near the stop sign," he confirms.

Since I've heard John describe the spot to Arnie, I now know where we're going. All too often, I follow John obliviously, sometimes losing track of where I am.

"Yup. Meet us there?"

"Probably," replies Jim. "Theo's a good place for burls."

Jim constructs furniture from log burls, using the large swirled defects in fallen timber to produce beautiful coffee tables. His extensive background in logging makes him a wood expert. Approaching 80-years-old, he shows no sign of slowing down.

We rumble out of the gas station. I've moved into John's truck for the ride, jammed against the passenger door by Bro, who stretches out in the center of the seat. Margy follows in her truck, towing our quads. Jim is still back at the gas station, and Arnie is who-knows-where.

* * * * *

We travel north on Highway 101, turning off at Southview Road. Then we drive up the dirt road to our planned turnout. Arnie is already parked and off-loaded, so he has managed to return home, load his quad in his truck, and beat us here – somehow. As Margy pulls in behind John's truck, Jim rolls up right behind her. Within a matter of a few minutes, a scattered group of riders arrive at the same spot.

Margy and I begin unfastening the straps that secure our quads to the trailer. Meanwhile, John walks over to talk with Arnie. I join them and introduce myself. When I explain to him this is the first ride for Margy's new bike, he gives me a blank stare, as if I'm giving him some kind of excuse. In fact, it's just that. If he's ridden with John before, he's used to a fast pace (even with Bro in his aft box). Now he'll know why we're slowing down the parade, as if a new bike really needs to go slow for break-in. But I feel better mentioning it.

Margy climbs onto her new silver quad, still atop the trailer, and John comes over to give her a checkout on the controls and switches before her first engine start. She's ridden my Kodiak 450 previously, and this one has exactly the same setup. But it's been a long time, and she's not about to turn down some training by John. In fact, I cram over against John, looking over his shoulder to see what I can learn.

Margy opens the choke, turns on the key, verifies the bike is in *Park*, and hits the green button. The quad starts smoothly. While she warms up her bike, I load my aft storage box. Then I climb aboard my Kodiak, set the controls, and hit the green starter button. Nothing.

I rock the bike to assure it's in *Park*, check the switches on the handlebars, and try again. Still nothing. Meanwhile, I hear Margy shift into reverse, and I turn in my seat to watch her back her bike off the trailer.

Surely this is operator error, so I stare at the switches again, most of which have nothing to do with starting the quad. When another attempt doesn't rotate the starter, I shift into neutral and try again. Finally, I decide it's time to get John's help.

"Hey, now it's my turn for some training in getting my bike started!" I yell to John.

He finishes backing his Grizzly out of his truck and down the metal ramps to the ground.

"Yuh, right!" he yells. "Start it up."

"I'm serious. Nothing happens when I hit the starter button."

"What gear are you in?" he asks.

"Neutral, but I tried starting in park, too."

John walks over to the trailer where I'm perched on top of my quad. He stands chest-high with my handlebars, looking down at my control settings. He immediately reaches in front of me and flips a red lever on my left handlebar.

"Try it now," he says.

Vroom! Vroom!

Problem solved.

"What?" I say.

"The kill switch," he says. "It cuts off your ignition."

"I swear I've never seen that switch before," I cringe.

"Better learn it now," he says, and promptly walks away.

I hope Arnie hasn't been paying attention.

I back off the trailer, park my bike behind Margy's, and take a picture of her on the new silver quad. While framing the photo, I think about the kill-switch, admitting to myself I didn't even know I had one. Without John, I would never have gotten my quad off the trailer. It's undoubtedly wise for him to be with us for Margy's break-in ride.

* * * * *

Margy drives away first, which is a change of pace for us. She drives around the corner, and I hear her stop. I guess she wants to make sure her new bike drives forward as well as starts.

I depart the off-load area next, stopping around the corner next to Margy. Arnie zips past us, speeding off towards Theodosia, and

Jim follows close behind. John and Bro are last, stopping when they come abeam Margy and me. We are ready first, John is ready last – something is weird about this day.

"Let's go!" says John, accelerating out onto the dirt road.

Margy falls into line behind John, and I bring up the rear. It's a near-perfect day for riding, with the morning clouds now nearly all gone. For August, it's remarkably cool, with an expected high of only 22. After two days of rain, the roads are still moist, which will suppress the dust that normally aggravates the comfort of summer rides on dirt roads. Today, we can ride right behind each other.

I slow tentatively and look both ways as I pass the stop sign in the middle of nowhere. To the right, the road leads up into the Bunster Range, and to the left is Okeover Inlet. I've yet to see another vehicle at this wilderness intersection.

When we come to the turn leading to the trail to Theodosia, Jim and Arnie are waiting for us. Arnie is using a small air compressor, powered by his quad's DC receptacle, to pump up one of his tires.

"Just a little low. Nothing serious," he says, as I drive up and stop beside him.

Jim pulls away almost immediately, off for Theodosia. John turns to Arnie to assure he's okay.

"No problem. I'll catch up," says Arnie.

John leads us along a mostly-downhill trail that quickly turns into a mix of rocky patches and stretches of muddy water about six inches deep. In low gear, using our engines for braking, we drop down the steep granite-strewn trail without need for four-wheel drive.

Margy and I reach the beginning of the narrow, winding trail that climbs over the ridge separating us from the Theodosia Valley. John has pulled over there, waiting for us. This is one of three trails into Theo. It's now the primary entrance, since the other main trail has been deactivated with deep trenches. The third route, the Last Chance Trail, is an indirect route to Theodosia, and it's a wicked path through tough terrain in the Bunsters. As John tells me: "You're not ready for that one – yet."

As we sit at the entrance to the trail, Arnie catches up, and John waves him around us. Arnie barely slows down, climbing the lower section of the trail expertly, and out of sight in just a few moments.

John raises his arm and holds up four fingers. It's time for four-wheel drive. He pulls away first, up the steep slope towards the top. Margy follows, using the luxury of her new four-wheel drive to climb slowly and steadily up the hill.

We're immediately in thick forest, winding through a park-like setting of big trees. This is one of my favourite trails, reminding me of a national park, but one requiring four-wheel drive. The trees are closely spaced, and the path winds continuously around them as we climb towards the top of the ridge.

Halfway through, we meet Jim, who has pulled off to the side of the trail, inspecting the forest. John yells something to him as he passes, then Margy goes past him, too. I stop to find out what Jim's doing.

"Look at the burls," he says. "This spot is like an oasis for old twisted wood."

He points to the other side of the trail, towards a huge tree where a large burl is bulging out halfway up the trunk. Then I walk with him to a spot where he has found a fallen log with a smaller burl, still a nice specimen.

After I leave Jim, I climb the rest of the way without stopping. When I pull out of the thick trees at the crest, Margy and John are off their bikes, and Bro is sniffing in the bushes nearby.

From here we'll ride an easy road straddling the ridge between the inlets of Lancelot and Theodosia, then through a rough trail leading down to the Theodosia logging dock. The last portion of the trail will be the biggest test of Margy's new bike. She has ridden this section on her old two-wheel drive quad, but she needed to have John take her bike through the steep section near the bottom.

Today, Margy conquers the steepest part of the trail near the dock without any problems. When we pull down the final few metres to the turnout at the bottom, Arnie is waiting for us. This is a traditional spot for a break before we continue our travel onto Theodosia Main, which will lead us through the valley.

We get off our bikes, and walk down the ramp to the logging dock, empty today even though it's a weekday. A logger's strike has been in effect for a full month, and it's strange to see this major logging area empty of activity. All of the big logging equipment is still here, sitting idle, but no workers are present.

Standing on the logging dock, we look across the inlet. A jumble of logs spreads out into the water, left rafted in the booms when the strike began.

Clouds hang low to the north, but it has turned out to be a mostly sunny day, perfect for fishing. Of course, this isn't the perfect spot, but I have my collapsible rod with me, so I pull it out. A large spoon is already attached, so I decide to use it. My first few casts produce no results, so I decide to go deeper. As John watches, I let my hook settle farther to the bottom.

"Don't go so deep," he suggessts. "Lots of cables and wood at the bottom here. You'll lose your lure," he says.

"I've got more red-and-white daredevils," I say.

In fact, I have a lot of these lures. This one, however, is bigger than most. And it has an inverted colour scheme. Unlike the standard red-and-white, it's reversed in colour, with more white than red. And it's my favourite.

Sure enough – I have no sooner ignored John's comments than I snag the bottom and lose my favourite spoon. So I attach a smaller

lure and offer the pole to Arnie. He tries a few casts, without any bites. Then he gives the pole back to me.

I drop the daredevil directly over the edge of the dock, letting it settle to the bottom. I jig a few times, making big pulls on the line.

"Watch out," says John. "You'll get snagged again."

Almost immediately, I catch a small greenling, a "Tommy" cod.

"Well, look who wins the contest today," I say.

"But you hooked him on the bottom," says John. "That's too easy."

Sometimes, between John and me, it's a constant verbal battle over anything we can think of. Call it a friendly skirmish, which John always wins.

* * * * *

We ride past the turnoff to Rupert's Farm. Arnie is behind John, followed by Margy, and then me. Jim is somewhere behind us, maybe not to be seen for the rest of the day. After a few kilometres, John leads us off the main onto a new logging road that climbs along the side a mountain, leading up to a large slash.

On the way up, in wide-open sunny patches, the slope below the road is covered with bright-purple fireweed in full bloom. On the slope above the road, the fireweed is past bloom. I can't figure out why these flowers bloom on such a different schedule so near to each other. The sunlight they receive seems to be the same, but the flow of ground water is probably different, interrupted by the road.

Margy slows during one precipitous stretch, but she doesn't stop. This is a major improvement since her bout of "quad acrophobia" I documented in *Up the Main* (Chapter 10). I'm sure John sees this and is mentally recording her percentile score.

When we reach the top of the slash, we pull into a turnout, get off our quads, and walk to the edge of the drop-off. Below us, on this side of the slash, is Olsen's Lake, although the slope is so steep we can't see it directly below. To the left (northwest), the Theodosia River tumbles downward past the lake. Several waterfalls run off the nearby mountains, somewhat of a rarity in August. Olsen's Creek winds to our right, (southeast), dropping towards Powell Lake.

We try to eat the lunches we've packed, but the mosquitoes give us no rest. They insistently buzz around our heads, making this beautiful spot less appealing. I walk over to the other side of the slash, just a few hundred metres farther along the road, where I can look down on Powell Lake. The wide bay just south of Olsen's Landing on the Goat Island side catches the glint of the afternoon sun, and I'm able to recognize several cabins I know.

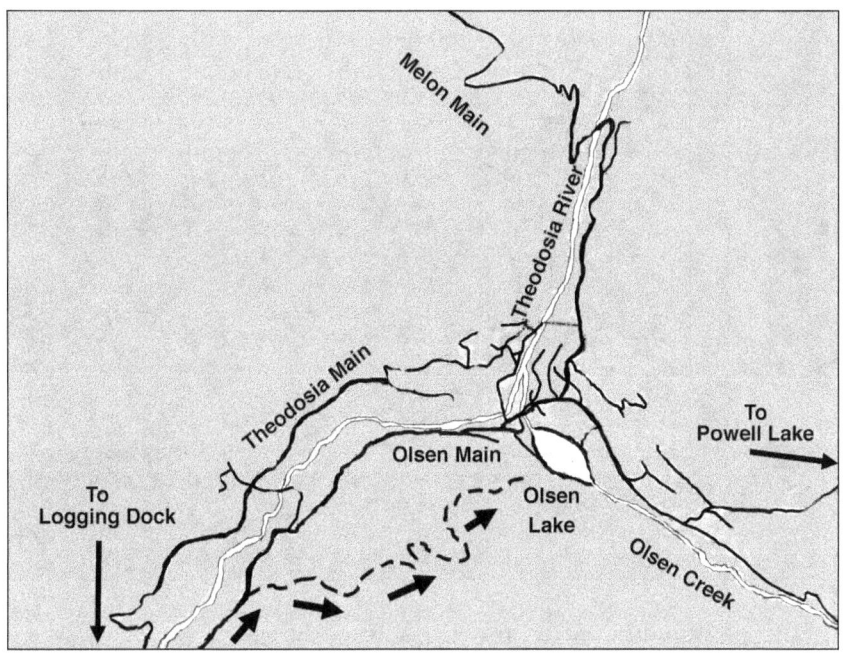

At another spot near the top of the slash, still swatting mosquitoes, we're able to look southwest towards Theodosia Inlet and the ocean beyond. Savary Island and the Copelands are easily visible, making this a mountaintop slash with a view of nearly 360 degrees. Of course, it takes a few steps in each direction, dodging bugs as much as possible, to obtain that perspective.

I put my helmet back on to ward off the mosquitoes. We're all anxious to get going and out of the relentless swarm. We start back down, and after the first kilometre, we again reach the stretch of road with fireweed. The view looking down the road is even more spectacular than it was on the way up. The trail hugs the side of the mountain, and I can look down and see Margy's quad in front of me, poised at the next hairpin turn.

Back on Theodosia Main once again, we cruise towards the logging dock and the trail out of the valley. I've asked John to stop at the intersection with Heather Main. On my list of things to do in the future is a trip to my floating cabin on Powell Lake via quad. It can be accomplished by a long ride from Theodosia Valley on Heather Main. He shows me the obvious (but unmarked) intersection, and I linger there a few minutes with thoughts of a self-guided quad ride to my

cabin, spending the night, and riding back the next day.

After leaving this intersection, it's a short hop to Rupert's Farm, deserted for decades. On the way into the farm, John shows me the shallow creek where salmon congregate during spawning season. The migration will begin any day now, but there are no fish here today. I'd like to return soon to see the salmon run upstream, although it's hard to imagine big salmon struggling through this shallow water.

We pause at the old barn, now partially renovated by quad riders as a covered picnic area. Then we head out to a field where abandoned farm vehicles sit in historic silence. We stop to test Margy's new winch. John and Arnie give her some practice by attaching her hook onto one of the derelict vehicles. But the winch's clutch won't release properly. Margy can run the winch out slowly and then retract it with the expected force, but the clutch mechanism is defective. Thus, the winch provides the only break-in snag on this "first ride," and it's only a minor problem.

After leaving Rupert's Farm and pulling back out onto Theodosia Main, John stops so we can catch up. He tells us he wants to visit one more spot before leaving the valley.

"I'd like to stop one more time to check out the ocean," he says.

No problem, but what does this mean? Theodosia Inlet is salt water, and it and Okeover are the only ocean water we'll pass on our return to the trucks. It strikes me as strange when John says it this way. Why does he want to see the ocean? None of us say anything, but we all nod, and off we go.

I fall a little behind, with all the other quads out of sight in front of me. As I drive along the main where it parallels the shore of Theodosia Inlet, I look for prospective side-roads where John might have turned off to the water. I know of two specific locations that are good lookout spots for the inlet, so I slow as I approach these turnoffs. I expect John to wait for me at such an intersection to assure I find it, but I pass both turns with no sign of him. So I continue all the way to the end of the road. I'm certain John wouldn't start up the trail out of the valley without waiting for me. Maybe he has changed his mind about "checking out the ocean."

At the end of the road, all three quads are parked, everyone standing around waiting for me. I pull up next to Margy and turn off my quad.

"Let's go down to the dock," says John.

A large yacht, rare in this inlet, rides at anchor a half-kilometre off the end of the dock. A seal snorts nearby, surfacing and swimming towards shore. Bro doesn't even hesitate – he's in the water immediately, dog-paddling towards the seal.

John notices what Bro is trying to do, but says nothing. If Bro catches the seal, I know who'll win the battle. The seal has some abilities a dog doesn't, including holding his breath nearly indefinitely, and I fear for Bro.

"Do you think Bro will be okay with a seal?" I ask.

"Probably," says John. "He'll never catch him."

Who'll never catch whom?

I unfold my fishing pole, and cast the puny red-and-white as far as I can. Almost immediately I feel a sharp pull on the line.

"Got one!" I yell. "Oh, it might be a snag."

As I wind in my line, I'm convinced it's not a fish.

"Might be a starfish," I say.

"That's not a fish, so it doesn't counts," notes John.

As if I didn't know.

When I finally pull my lure to the surface, a slab of bark is on the hook. I plop it onto the dock.

"A bark fish," John says. "About the same size as the other one."

The piece of bark lies on the dock, looking remarkably fish-shaped. But it's definitely wood.

"So it proves what a great fisherman I am," I say.

"Big time," says John.

I hand the pole to Arnie, satisfied this is the best I can do with a fishing pole today.

John and I stretch out flat on our backs on the hard wooden surface. The firm deck feels good on my back, and the sun beams down to warm my body in a most pleasant way. Arnie continues to fish while we lie on the dock. Bro is still splashing around close to shore, looking for seals. Margy steps back and captures a photo of men at work.

◊ ◊ ◊ ◊ ◊ ◊ ◊

Chapter 5

Rain Turnin' to Snow

"It's hard to say what's going to happen with the weather," says John, as I talk to him over the telephone on Friday night. "Call me in the morning at eight-thirty."

"That early?" I ask. "I don't want to wake anybody up."

"Not me. I'll be up."

Since when? John seldom gets up before nine o'clock, and we never start out on a ride any earlier. But the days are getting short in mid-November, so we'll need to get going early, if we get going at all.

The weather forecast for the weekend is marginal, but we'll take what we can get. After a full week of rain, I'd like to try a ride, if it isn't pouring. There seems little harm in what is forecast: cloudy with light rain most of the day. After all, we've got rain gear.

Early the next morning, the view from the condo patio looks promising. The barely-risen sun is hidden behind high clouds, with a few blue breaks over Vancouver Island. The television weather forecast still calls for light rain, but it isn't raining yet. And the next day shows a forecast of showers, which could be better, but could also be worse. Things are day-to-day in November, with forecasts not to be trusted. I feel we should go for it, but I know John hates to ride in the rain.

When I call John from McDonald's at 8:30, he answers on the first ring: "You're up already," I say.

"Told you I would be. Looks crappy outside."

"I know, but Margy and I want to go riding anyway, even if it rains a little. We can go by ourselves, so you decide what you want to do."

"Do you have your trailer hooked up yet?" he asks.

"No, we're just doin' a breakfast drive-through now, so we'll get the trailer next."

"Call me when you're all hooked up, and we'll know more about the weather by then."

Already I'm feeling guilty. John isn't going to be pleased if I get him out in the bush and it starts to rain. Although I prefer to have him lead us on a ride, this seems like the kind of day when we're best on our own. Then if it rains, Margy and I can continue or simply give up and head back to town. To waste John's time on this seems unfair. He hates short rides, and he hates the rain, and a combination seems likely today.

After hooking up to the quad trailer at the airport, we start down Duncan Avenue towards John's house. A few small drops of rain are already hitting the windshield. While Margy drives, her cell phone rings, so I answer it. Not surprisingly, it's John.

"Where are you?" he asks.

"Bearing down on you right now," I say. "About two minutes out, and inbound like a rocket. But Margy and I think you should let us go quadding by ourselves. You don't need to ride around in the rain."

"Okay, you go by yourself," he says, sounding relieved. "But you're gonna get wet."

"Hey, we're from Los Angles, so we're brave. Stupid, too."

John laughs. I think he sometimes forgets what a different environment we're from. Rain, to us, is exciting.

"Where are you planning to go?" he asks.

"Standby – we're making a low pass by your house right now. Take a look."

Margy turns off the main street, and we pass right by John's house. I reach over and honk the horn as we continue down the road towards the alley where we'll turn so we can circle around and head back north of town.

"There goes your trailer!" says John.

He's just like a kid, and so am I – we have fun just driving around, honking horns, and yelling: "I see you!"

"We're considering going to Mud Lake, off-loading at the normal spot, and then riding up to Granite Lake. Or maybe up Mount Mahony. What do you think?"

"You need to get up into the snow," says John. "It's a lot better than rain, though you'll eventually have to come back down. You won't see snow at Granite Lake today. And Mount Mahony won't have any until you're near the top."

John knows this region. He can calculate snow levels with a quick look at the thermometer, along with his vast knowledge of the local geography.

"In any case, we'll head north," I say. "Hey, stand by for another low pass."

We've completed our trip down the alley and are back on the street, about to pass by his house again. *Honk! Honk! Honk!*

"There you go!" John yells into the telephone.

"We're outta here," I say.

We're gone, and headed north.

* * * * *

We drive towards Cranberry, to keep our options open. After hanging up the phone, Margy and I discuss another possibility. We could still turn east from Cranberry and head towards Mud Lake, or we could veer off towards Mount Mahony. But now we're considering turning west instead, over to Highway 101, and north towards the Bunster Range. We've been there in the snow before, and the climb is on a good forestry road. Although John didn't mention the Bunsters, it seems we might be able to climb high enough to get out of the rain, which is now falling more heavily.

"Which way?" I ask, as we slow approaching the stop sign in Cranberry.

"Left," says Margy.

"Sounds good to me," I reply, as Margy turns on her left turn signal.

When we ride by ourselves, we never have a problem agreeing on destinations. Anything works for us. We just like to ride and explore. It really matters little where we go.

We join Highway 101, cross the bridge below the Shinglemill, and drive north through Sliammon to Wilde Road, where we turn inland and start a gradual climb towards the Bunsters. Wilde Road transitions into Thomkinson Road and then to the forest service road, where it begins to get a little rough. Margy slows to allow our trailer to ride easier under the weight of our two quads. It's a good trailer, but dirt roads can shake things enough to throw off cargo straps.

Our favourite off-load spot is a mud hole today. It looks like we can get off the road here, but we won't be able to back down the spur and turn around. So we elect to drive a bit farther and see what happens.

Almost immediately, branches are strewn all along the road. This always seems to be an area where wind leaves its mark, and today is no exception. Two recent back-to-back storms have blown down several trees that have already been cut free of the road. Somebody, probably a recreational rider with a chainsaw, has reopened the road.

"No farther," says Margy, as a fallen tree appears ahead, partially blocking the road.

"I think you can get by," I reply.

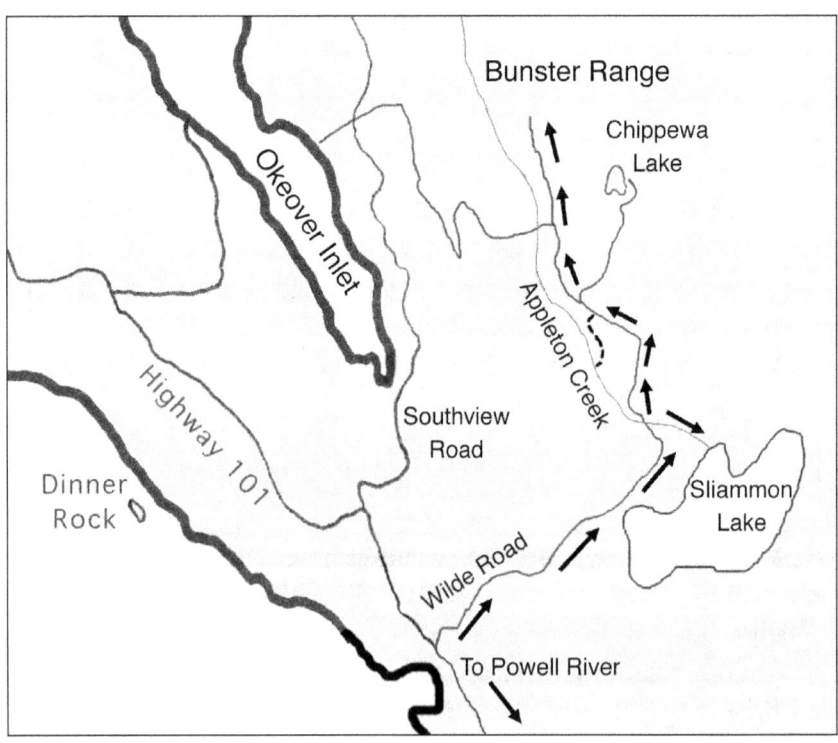

Margy tries to edge past the tree. The truck gets a bit too close to the edge of the road, and her tires start to spin in the mud. Shifting into four-wheel drive, we get going again and ease past the rut we've created. Beyond the tree, we find a turnout that appears good-enough to off-load, particularly since we don't expect anything better ahead.

The rain is falling hard enough for us to reconsider our plans before going through the work of off-loading the trailer. It's an easy decision.

"You feel okay with the rain?" I ask.

"Sure," replies Margy. "It's a warm rain, and we can always turn around and come back."

"Let's go up as high as we feel comfortable before we turn around. Maybe we'll find some snow."

"Sliammon Lake for lunch?"

"If I can wait that long. We can stop at the upper portion of the Appleton Creek trail, too. According to the map, there's a campsite near the creek."

Lunch is always a priority. I used to laugh at John when he would carry a lunch (or two) wherever he went. But soon I came to realize

that off-road riding or hiking makes a lunch stop a requirement. Being stranded a few times with John, watching him eat his lunch, taught me to always pack some food. I'm not sure where the energy is expended, especially when pushing the thumb-throttle of a quad, but it doesn't take a long ride to make a lunch stop a necessity.

I suit up for the ride, including rain pants that slip reluctantly over my heavy boots. I'm wearing four layers now, which may be a bit too hot for the trip, especially when we get off our quads and hike.

My cheap gloves are thick and warm, but not rainproof. Before we begin to off-load our bikes, I put on my helmet, the perfect rain hat, and begin to unstrap the quads.

"Let's look for a turnaround spot up the road," I say. "If we don't find one, we can always disconnect the trailer before we reload it with the quads, and turn the truck around right here."

"I'd prefer that," says Margy. "It looks awfully tight to try backing up with the trailer. Ditches on both sides too."

We tend to agonize over finding the perfect spot for off-loading. In reality, it's a simple matter to remove the empty trailer from the tow hitch and swing the truck around separately. But it's a nice luxury to simply leave them connected, ramps down and ready to receive our quads when we return from a ride.

In a few minutes, we're riding up the dirt road in the rain, now pelting at my helmet because of our forward speed. Goggles with an anti-fog lens keep most of the water off my face. A few drops make it down my cheek, trickling along my neck, but it's hardly noticeable. A cold rain would be different, but I'm hoping we find snow before it gets uncomfortable. Riding in the snow always feels a lot drier, and surprisingly warmer.

I follow Margy, letting her set the pace for the climb. We don't find any good turnouts for the truck until we reach the road winding down to Sliammon Lake. We pull off there to reevaluate.

"No good turnoffs until here," I say. "And this is too far to bring the truck."

"Just as easy to turn around back there," says Margy.

"You still okay with the rain?" I ask.

"Fine," she says. "If it doesn't pour any harder, I could ride like this all day."

I'm not sure I feel the same, but the rain isn't a problem for now. As we climb higher, the bombardment on my helmet gets noisier; bigger drops, maybe even a little grauple – freezing rain forming tiny ice chunks on the way down. I catch a glimpse of white streaks intermixed with clear drops. The rain is turning to snow.

We stop at the sign by the side of the road that designates *Nature Trail*, with an arrow marked *Appleton Creek*.

"This spot isn't as easy to find on the way down the hill," I note. "Coming up the road, like this, it jumps out and grabs you. It'd be nice to stop here and walk the trail, if the rain quits on the way back down."

"Let's find some landmarks around the corner, so we don't miss it on the way back," suggests Margy. "Does it seem like the rain is turnin' to snow?"

"I can't see it here, but I caught a glimpse of some flakes while we were riding back there, or maybe some ice pellets."

"Me too," says Margy. "But right here it's definitely rain, and not very cold."

We continue up the road, now more rutted but still an easy route for a quad. I make note of a large culvert passing under the main at an oblique angle. It'll be a good reference marker on the way back down, to make sure we don't miss the trail to Appleton Creek.

We pass the spur to Chippewa Lake, while streaks of white now swirl all around my helmet. This time, it's definitely snow, with large flakes splashing onto my goggles and quickly melting.

By the time we reach the junction where the Bunster Range trail joins the main, just before the bridge over Appleton Creek, it's more snow than rain – but still not completely turned. A few patches of old snow are scattered along the road, but there's no evidence snow has been significant here yet this year.

At the bridge, we meet two other riders, headed down towards Sliammon Lake. One of them drives a red Honda three-wheeler, the predecessor of today's quad, now over thirty years old. This is the "trike" that led the revolution in off-road transportation, with an infamous roll-over record that nearly killed the sport. Still, I marvel at this bike. It's beautifully restored and obviously cherished by its owner.

"Careful, it might snow," I kid the three-wheel rider as we pull off to the side to let the two bikes pass.

"Too late. It already is," says the fellow on the red trike. "It's all rain back towards Okeover."

After the riders pass, I pull forward onto the bridge and stop, looking down at the rushing waters tumbling from the Bunsters towards Sliammon Lake. It's a mix of roaring whitewater pouring over smoothly eroded reddish-brown rocks.

Off to the side of the road, next to the bridge, a white pickup truck is parked, with quad ramps spread out behind. Maybe other riders are on the trail to the Bunster Range today.

My experience on this trail is snow deepening rapidly as you climb higher, even though the elevation gain doesn't appear significant. Throughout winter, the Bunster Range is covered in white, while nearby areas remain in the rain. As a moist airmass pushes in from the chuck, the Bunsters abruptly boost the air upward, condensing quickly into snow.

We enter the trail, Margy in the lead. We wind gradually uphill, brush-high alders whacking against our helmets. Almost immediately, the remaining rain turns completely to snow. It's that quick.

The ground is still wet, but in only a few hundred metres, the trail is covered with a thin layer of white. As we continue up the trail, the snowfall is light but marked by fast flakes streaking past my goggles. The snowy path shows the tracks of a vehicle ahead, and in another half-kilometre we meet the quad, headed back down the trail. A man with a snow-covered helmet drives, with a woman riding on the back, along with a rear rack full of small branches, maybe gathered for wreaths. They pull off to the side of the trail to allow us to pass. We nod *Hello* as we go by, exchanging smiles, and then we continue up the trail in the rapidly deepening snow.

I'm always amazed how fast the snow deepens while climbing the Bunsters. Although it's still mid-November, we could get stuck here, after traveling only a few hundred metres from the main road.

Getting mired down in the snow in a quad is more of a challenge than a problem. Your options include using your winch (or another quad's winch) to pull yourself out. Our Kodiak 450s are light enough for two people to rock them out of most situations, and there's four-wheel drive and even differential lockers.

"Stay in two-wheel drive," I say to Margy, when she pulls off to the side to discuss whether we should continue farther. "That way we won't be tempted to go past our limit with four-wheel drive."

"Okay," she replies. "I'm almost at my limit now."

"Let's see if we can make it to the logging slash."

The slash is near the top of the main trail, where the Last Chance Trail begins. Someday I'll try that demanding trail, but not today – and not without John.

We make it to the slash easily, still trucking ahead in two-wheel drive. We turn around at a spur that gives us lots of space, and stop for a first-of-the-season snow photo.

"What would John do in a situation like this?" I ask.

"He'd keep on driving until he was totally stuck," says Margy. "Only then would he turn around."

It's true. John loves to push on until he can go no farther, then struggle with extracting his quad from the snow. Often that means using a winch. For me, on the other hand, I'm satisfied to stop well short of my limit. Both scenarios are safe. Mine is lazier.

After a short break stomping around in the snow, we drive back down the trail towards the main road. Our uphill tracks have already been completely covered by the new snow. It's not a whiteout, but snow accumulates fast here. And it feels comfortably warm and dry, though I'm glad I'm wearing multi-layers today.

Only my hands are cold, reminding me that waterproof gloves would be a wise investment. I wring my hands, and water drips from the soaked material. Fortunately, it's not winter-cold today.

Riding back down the forestry road, it's raining again, though still light. As snow melts from my helmet, it slides down my visor in mushy globs, then splashes onto my jacket.

When we cross the angled culvert, I release the thumb pressure on my throttle. In front of me, Margy has already slowed nearly to a halt, looking for the entrance to the nature trail, which we easily find. Pulling our quads to the side of the road, Margy removes her helmet, and gets off her bike. Her long hair slides down over her wet jacket.

"Hey, where's your hat?" I ask.

"Back at the truck."

"Mine too," I reply. "Use your helmet. It makes a good rain hat."

So we begin the climb up the wide path leading to the narrower Appleton Creek trail, both of us wearing our helmets. It may look silly, but it keeps our heads dry. Besides, who's going to see us?

We follow the well-marked trail to the footbridge crossing a small tributary of Appleton Creek. Then we hike mostly uphill, encountering lots of small trees that have fallen across the trail during recent storms.

I lead, pulling the smaller trunks and branches out of the way. We climb over the bigger blow-downs, trudge through some areas where the wind damage is more extensive, and follow the trail until it levels and begins descending towards Appleton Creek. Even through my helmet, the roar of the water below is evident.

When we sight the footbridge over the creek, we leave the main trail and deviate down to the bridge and its adjacent campsite. It's a

beautiful spot, with a giant old-growth fir poised next to a picnic table. I try taking a photo with my camera, but the lens is completely fogged. Often, the best images are in your mind, and cannot be captured in a picture anyway.

We consider hiking all the way down the Appleton Creek Trail (a segment of the Sunshine Coast Trail) to the main road, then walking back up the main to retrieve our bikes. But the sign here says: *Wilde Road 2.1 kilometres*, a pretty good hike since it doesn't include the steep walk back up the road to our quads. We'll try that hike sometime soon, but next time we'll approach it more efficiently by leaving a quad at the south entrance to the trail. Then, at the end of the hike, we can "double" to our other quad at the trail's north entrance. It's a lazy way, but much more resourceful.

So today we hike back out the same way we came in, rain still falling when we arrive back at our quads. From there, we travel down the main, pulling off at Sliammon Lake and parking under a tree for protection from the drizzle. When we walk out onto the granite cliff overlooking the lake, the rain has nearly stopped. The water dripping from the trees is worse than out in the open.

Here, on the shore, we eat our lunch, near the end of a short trip (31 kilometres, not including the hike) that was totally enjoyable, even in a persistent rain turning to snow. I look out over the unspoiled beauty of the tree-lined lake. It's only a brief ride back to the truck, but what would a quad ride be without lunch? John would have liked this part, and he'd also have enjoyed the snow. He wouldn't, however, have liked riding in the rain.

Chapter 6

Pickin' Apples

I wave goodbye to the Pacific Coastal Beech 1900C as it pulls out of its parking spot in front of the Powell River terminal. I don't know if Margy is on this side of the airplane, but I wave anyway. When the twin-turboprop completes its turn towards the runway, I wave again for the passengers on the other side.

The aircraft wastes no time entering the runway for its back-taxi to Runway 27. I walk to the truck, nearly ready to head back up the lake. I'll need some groceries and a quick stop at the condo to pick up a few things. Then I'll be gone. But first, I telephone John.

"Hey, do you hear an airplane taking off?" I say, as soon as John answers the phone.

"No, nothing here," he says.

"Listen again. Here it comes."

The twin-Beech is just now breaking ground, climbing out over John's house.

"There it is," says John. "Pacific Coastal."

"Margy's flying," I say.

"Yeah, right."

"Why not. She's a pilot, and they let just about anybody fly."

"Right."

"So what are you doing today?" I ask, knowing this drizzly rain will keep him off the trails.

"Well, I was going to Mount Alfred, but now I think I'll take my truck and go pick some apples."

"Fiddlehead?"

"If it isn't too early for apples. Got four bags last year at the end of August."

"I didn't know you like apples," I reply. "It's a fruit, you know?"

Fruits and vegetables aren't on John's menu, unless disguised by meat and potatoes.

"It's somethin' to do," replies John. "Too wet to take my quad."

"How about going apple pickin' in the new truck rather than the old one?" I ask.

"Sure," he says.

"I'll be there in half an hour."

* * * * *

Margy's truck is far from new, but it's newer than John's Ford. John has taken his old truck to amazingly remote locations, although his off-road travel in recent years has been mostly by quad. Before his Grizzly 660, he hammered a big Honda motorcycle on every trail in the region. The weather forecast for today is more palatable in a truck, with the probability of precipitation at 60 percent. Tomorrow's POP is 70 percent, and the following day shows only rain. August is ending the way summer began – cool and wet. This is the year, 2008, some describe as the year without a summer. (The following summer, 2009, set records for its high temperatures and an almost total lack of rain.)

Apple picking wasn't in my plans today, but maybe I can still make it up the lake before dark. A trip with John is seldom a simple, short affair, but it's only 9:15 in the morning, so I figure we should be home well before dark. I know our ride to Fiddlehead Farm won't be a direct route, since that's not the way John travels. But in the truck, I'll be able to get some good hints for future quad trips, a difficult process when I ride with him on our quads. When we're on our separate bikes, we can't talk (without yelling) as we ride. In a truck, with John right next to me, I gather lots of trail information. Besides, its interesting to ponder how John will get to Fiddlehead by truck, a trip that would be challenging for me even on a quad.

It takes me nearly an hour to do the errands that must be completed if I'm going to make it up the lake later today. If we get back to town after 5 pm, most of the stores will be closed. Evening business hours haven't made it to this part of the coast.

When I pull into John's driveway, my promised half-hour has expired, so he's waiting for me. The driveway is full of equipment that's ready to go – long pike poles to reach overhanging branches, bags for the apples, lunch, chainsaw, and toolbox. Maybe this won't be a quick trip, after all.

I help John load his stuff into the truck's back canopy, while Bro runs around pretending to help. When John heads for the driver's door, I walk up behind them.

"Shall I drive?" I ask.

The answer is obvious. I really can drive a truck. It's just that John always drives, whether it's a car, boat, or truck. We all prefer it that way.

"Okay, you can drive," he says, as he slips into the driver's seat.

I walk around to the passenger door, where Bro waits for a doorman. The big Lab leaps in, and does a quick and awkward circle in the seat, inspecting his assigned space. I have to push him to the center so there's room for me. Bro is used to his customary position as number one passenger. But all the seats in the "new" truck are cushy, so he accepts the center spot.

We ride south on Route 101, turning off at Dixon Road. (A shorter route to Fiddlehead Farm, at least by quad, is north along Haslam Lake.) Then we travel up the dirt road to the split in Goat Main. In the bushes at the side of the intersection, I can barely read the mostly-covered sign: *One-Way*, with an arrow to the left.

"Look at that sign," I say. "I wonder if a tourist would see it."

"Doubt it," replies John. "They'd probably go to the right here, and end up going backwards down a one-way road, right into the oncoming logging trucks."

"Serves 'em right," I say, but I'm sure John knows I'm kidding.

"Doesn't matter," replies John. "Everyone 'round here knows which way to go."

Good point. We don't need the signage; the tourists do, but the brush has taken over the sign. The danger is minimal right now, since the loggers have been on strike for over a month. Meanwhile, the logging roads are closing in fast from the sides – already overgrown in spots by alders. It's amazing how quickly the forest reclaims anything built by man.

We continue up the one-way portion of Goat Main to Tin Hat Junction, where two-way traffic (if there is any) resumes. In a few kilometres we are at the real Tin Hat junction, where you turn off Goat Main to go to Tin Hat Mountain. There's reason in this system of names, but I haven't figured it out yet.

We make our turn at this intersection, where Spring Lake Main splits off to the left. We continue uphill to a "Y," where a new main splits off to the right. We come to a stop here, while John looks up the new road.

"Never been on that road," says John.

It's a rarity. There is virtually nowhere in this area John hasn't traveled. But new logging roads are popping up all the time, while others fade away from disuse and encroachment by the forest. The new road even has a fresh wooden sign that reads *Lewis Lake Main*.

"Where does it go?" I ask.

"To Lewis Lake."

"Duh."

"But to the other side, not like the old road we're on now," he adds. "It follows an old railroad grade that takes you right to the lake from this side."

John has never been on this road, but he knows it's exact route. When we turn off on the road and he stops at a new bridge, I understand why.

"I was here with my truck, years ago," he explains. "Couldn't make it across this ravine, except by hiking down and thrashing through to the other side."

I look down to the rough canyon below. It's treacherous looking, covered by a dense growth of bushes and trees blocking the creek from view. I try to imagine hiking through such a mess.

"I followed the old railroad bed, all the way to Lewis Lake," he says. "Tough hike, but I was hoping to find an old steam locomotive buried around here somewhere. There are rumors about it, but I've never found it."

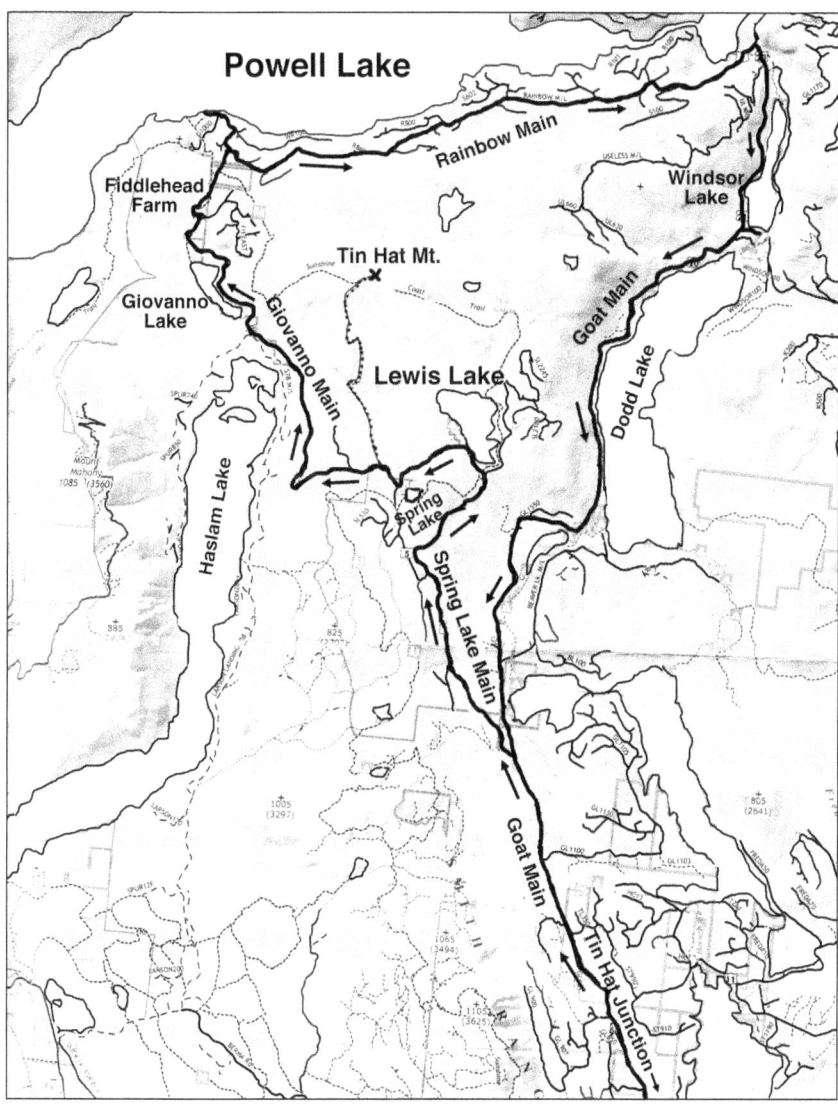

We cross the bridge and continue up Lewis Lake Main. In a half-kilometre, we come head-to-head with a pickup truck topped by a tall camper shell, the first traffic we've seen on the forest roads today. The driver stops in one of the few turnouts on the road, and we pass on by. If it weren't for the turnout, it would have been necessary for one of us to back up a long way to find another place to pass on this narrow, windy road.

We come to a sign marking the turnoff to the Lewis Lake campground. To our left is another sign, *SCT*, designating the Sunshine Coast Trail.

"That trail follows the railroad bed," says John. "We're on an old skid road now."

How does he know this? I've asked John how he accumulates so much knowledge of the local area. His reply: "Just by explorin' around for years and years, traveling everywhere I can."

Another narrow path splits off to the left, where John points the truck across a shallow trench. This trail would be easy on a quad, but I'd never try it in a truck. John comes to a halt, switches into four-wheel drive, and then continues forward.

"Feel that?" he asks, as he slowly maneuvers across the ditch.

"Barely," I reply.

I can feel, maybe hear, a slight scraping at the back of the truck as he eases up and out of the trench.

"It's the tow hitch," he says. "Not a problem, as long as I take it slow."

I can picture the extended bar of the towing hitch, barely touching the ground. John knows trucks, and he knows just how far to push them without hurting them. It's an art.

The trail is barely wide enough for our truck, but relatively smooth except for numerous shallow trenches. John points out a nearly invisible quad trail splitting off to the left. I'll want to try that path on my own someday soon. Then we pass a tiny lake to our right, nearly engulfed by the trees.

"That's Jimmy's lake," says John. "He just loves to fish there."

I would have guessed this lake, really only a pond, was too small to have any fish. But if Jimmy fishes here, it must be good fishing.

"Does it have a name?" I ask.

"Too small," replies John.

"Then we can call it Wayne's Lake," I kid.

"Jimmy wouldn't like that."

* * * * *

We pass Spring Lake, out of sight from our position on the trail, and rejoin the main. A sign labels it as *Giovanni Lake Main*.

"See!" says John, pointing to the sign. "Look how they spelled it."

Giovanni is the way we say it. *Giovanno* is how it usually appears on maps. But here they spelled it with an "i" at the end, which pleases John. Names in this region have evolved from traditional loggers' names for newly explored places. *Giovanni* can be *Giovanno* or *Frog Lake*. Everyone accepts the contradictions.

The main road winds past the head of Haslam Lake. We pause for a break at a scenic spot looking down on the water. As soon as Bro is out of the truck, he runs around like a mad man, hunting for critters in the bushes along the side of the road.

As we look down on the lake, clouds shroud the nearby ridges, and a shower hovers over nearby Mount Mahony. So far, we've encountered only a few sprinkles that stopped soon after they started, but it still could pour.

From here, it's a brief ride past Giovanni Lake, which is mostly shrouded in the trees below us. The water has a distinct greenish hue, a characteristic of the lake that persists even when you ride down to the shore. John shows me the turnoff for the quad trail leading to the

lake, and then we continue northbound on the narrow logging road. Here, the main is raised uncharacteristically high above deep trenches on both sides. You wouldn't want to slip a tire of your logging truck off the edge of this road. It would take a crane to get you out of the ditch.

We drop down into Fiddlehead Farm, once a prosperous little community for farming and wilderness tourism. Now, most of the old buildings have been demolished, and logging has slashed through the upper reaches of the former farm. Looking down the road, near the entrance, a white pickup truck pulls away in front of us.

"Grow op!" I suggest.

"Could be," says John. "But I doubt it. Probably just cutting alders."

The logging companies contract out for the removal of alders from slashes and along the mains, to allow the future growth of reforested sections. Alders are the scourge of the forests, overtaking the land everywhere they find open sunlight.

As we pass the spot where the white pickup departed, two boxes of commercial chemicals sit beside the road, along with some tools.

"They'll be coming back," says John. "They cut the bigger alders and try to kill the little ones with spray. But they just keep growing back."

Which is worse? – killing new growth, or allowing it to kill the newly planted trees? I can't decide, but the forest industry has.

We wind down to the meadow where five apple trees huddle in a small grove. The summer has been particularly wet, and this place is a reminder the weather hasn't been normal. It feels damp all around us, and the ground is visibly wet.

Pulling into the grassy area near the trees, we get stuck. But it's only a brief delay, as John switches into four-wheel drive and backs out.

We unload our apple picking equipment, and begin the task at hand. John uses a pike pole to reach upward to the top of the nearest tree, adeptly knocking some small apples to the ground.

"Taste one," says John, biting into a mottled red-and-green apple.

I notice he takes only a small bite, chews for a moment, and then spits it out. Then he hands the apple to me.

I taste it – not bad, but a bit tart, more like a crab apple than the full-sized store variety. We don't spend any time munching on apples. Instead, we get right to the task of harvesting the trees.

"A few marks on these apples is okay," says John. "As long as there aren't any worms. Using them for juice anyway."

So that explains it. John isn't going to eat apples. After all, it's a fruit. Instead, the apples will be ground up into juice by his mom. I should have known.

"Hear that?" asks John. "A quad – sounds like Rick."

When I listen carefully, I can hear the faint sound of a motor. John can tell the sound of a quad from a long distance, and he can identify many bikes by their specific sound.

"I hear it," I reply. "Do you really think it's Rick?"

"Probably," says John. "Look for a white helmet. Rick said he might try to find us."

The white helmet and the green Grizzly 700 appear right on schedule, wandering down the road into Fiddlehead. Rick pulls up near our truck, and I go over to meet him, while John continues to knock apples off the tree with his pole.

"Isn't it kind of wet on a quad today?" I ask Rick, when he turns off his engine.

No brother of John would ever ride in the rain, if he could avoid it.

"Not bad. Caught a shower back there, but it didn't last long."

The clouds around us harbour rain, and we all know it. Rick is out riding, hoping for the best, and trying to find us. It's something to do.

My job involves leaning over to pick up the apples from the ground, as John knocks them off the tree. I need to stay close to him, so I can see where the apples fall. Otherwise, many of them end up lost in the tall grass. This means I need to hover right below the action of John's pike pole. An occasional apple hits me, a few directly on my head. Fortunately, they are mostly small apples falling from low branches.

Down here, close to the ground and near the wet grass, it's hot and humid. Mosquitoes swarm around my sweating body, biting at will. After picking up two bags of apples, I'm ready for the project to be over. John's job is at least as hard, holding the long pole up for extended periods, whacking apples.

After three bags, John is still working on the last tree. I know he isn't going to be satisfied until we've collected every possible apple. And certainly he won't accept anything less than last year's record of four bags.

Rick and Bro are off exploring on their own, looking over the remains of the old buildings. When they return, I'm quick to complain to Rick that this apple picking could go on forever.

"He won't stop before you," says Rick. "It's just the way he is."

Finally, we are finished. John walks below the trees, finding a few apples I missed in the tall grass. Meanwhile, I take a break near a blackberry patch, where an endless supply of berries is available for the picking. I eat a few of the juicy treats, perfectly ripe this time of year. In late August, apples and blackberries go hand-in-hand.

We load five bags of apples into the truck, collect our equipment, and head for Powell Lake. Rick leaves in front of us, and we follow his quad tracks down to the water. But by the time we reach the parking area near the shore, Rick's tracks have sped off, after his brief stop.

John and I walk down to the empty logging dock, near the spot where the creek from Giovanni spills into Powell Lake. I pull out my collapsible fishing pole and try a few casts, but there are no bites. As usual, catching fish isn't so important to me. The relaxation provided by throwing in a line at a quiet spot and the joy of absorbing the scenery is the real prize.

Back in the truck, John leads me along Rainbow Main, the long way home. But this route will prevent duplication of our previous path, making it a more enticing round trip. Right away, I'm surprised by what I find on Rainbow Main – hoards of alders encroaching onto the road.

This logging road is one of the prettiest in the area, when the view down to Powell Lake is visible. When I last traveled Rainbow Main, only a year ago, it was wide open. Now it's a narrow path with alder branches brushing against both sides of the truck, and the lake is nearly invisible through the thick new trees. The forest has reclaimed the main line quickly.

After junctioning south on Goat Main, we ride past Windsor Lake to its outlet, where the water flows into Dodd Lake. We stop and walk to the south end of Windsor Lake along a portage for the Powell River Canoe Route. At the end of this short path, a small dock overlooks Windsor Lake.

I walk out on the dock and try casting with my white-and-red daredevil. The lure is a bit too big for most trout, but it might entice a large fish. At least, considering its heavy weight, I can cast it a long way.

Meanwhile, John and Bro hike closer to the lake's mouth, which requires clambering over logs jammed against the shore, and walking precariously along some that float in the shallow water. John and Bro walk boom logs effortlessly, but I elect to stay on the dock.

John finally makes it all the way to the outlet, while Bro returns near the dock to hunt for frogs. This will be our last stop before heading home down Goat Main and back to town. I should make it back up Powell Lake before dark, after all.

As for me, I snag my daredevil on an underwater log and have to break the line. But there are other lures, and other places, and other times to fish. For now, it's simply a place to enjoy on a showery August day.

Center-of-Book Photos

John (right) with Rick (and Bro) on Mount Mahony

On Blue Ridge above Haslam Lake

Theodosia River at Rupert's Farm

Theodosia Valley from Quad Point on Theodosia Inlet

Theodosia Valley Meadow

Margy Enters Theodosia Valley

Wayne with Danny and Kodiak 450s

Winter view looking east over Powell Lake from Heather Main

Chapter 7

Heather Main

One of the conveniences of quads is their use in camping. You can get to spots not accessible by other vehicles. But you have to carry what you need on your bike. Wouldn't it be nice to roll into a camping spot with everything already there?

If you own a floating cabin that's reachable by quad, what a solution! If only we could get to our cabin by quad. Indirectly, we can. But it takes some effort.

John has ridden to his cabin, directly across from ours, on his quad. One route, the Last Chance Trail over the Bunsters, is probably too difficult for me. The other more leisurely route is through Theodosia Valley on Heather Main, which in recent years has connected all the way through to Chippewa Bay. But this route has two main challenges: it has numerous unmarked spurs; and the final descent to Chippewa and Hole in the Wall is lengthy and complex. In other words, I have multiple opportunities to get lost.

Margy and I have traveled both ends of Heather Main with John, including snowshoe trips on both sides. The lengthy center section, although high and remote, will be new and exciting. Riders sometimes make the long round-trip ride in a single day, but we'll have the luxury of staying overnight at our cabin.

"How about a compromise?" asks John on the phone, the night before our planned departure.

I've been trying to convince John to accompany us on the ride, but the challenge of the route on our own is also enticing. So any compromise he wants should be fine.

"Sure. What do you have in mind?"

"If you feel comfortable on your own, I'll go up to Heather Main on the Last Chance Trail to meet you above Chippewa. Then I can lead you down."

The Last Chance Trail is a tough route for anyone, but if he's willing to take that shortcut to meet us, it would be a fun rendezvous.

"Sounds great. Of course, dependent upon weather," I add.

"Of course. Everything is."

This has been the year without a summer. Never before have I witnessed such a cool, rainy July and August. This week's forecast looks like more of the same.

"Let's see..." I say. "I'll give you an estimate of when we expect to be at the end of Heather Main, about to start down to Chippewa Bay, I'd say about 2 o'clock."

"Okay, nothing for sure. But we'll see what happens."

It's exactly the way we both like it.

* * * * *

That night, I preflight my chainsaw, getting it ready for the next day. Normally, I don't need to carry a saw, since John always carries one. But on this trip I'll be responsible for getting through any blow-downs along the way.

Behind the cabin, where my spare gas is stored, I refuel the saw in the dark, using a flashlight to complete the task. I add chain bar oil, wrap the saw in protective rags, and put it in the Campion.

The next morning, I'm up early, checking the weather. The forecast has gone downhill, but cool and damp is fine for riding. Only a persistent rain would be a problem. The precipitation forecast is sketchy: "Showers and sunny periods today," says the news broadcaster. It's worth a try – we can always turn back at any point in the lengthy process of traveling down the lake to town, hooking up to the quad trailer at the airport, driving to the off-load spot, and even after we're on the trail.

By 8:30 am, Margy and I are independently headed back into the Hole, me in the tin boat and Margy in the Campion. I deposit the tin boat for the shuttle back to our cabin later today. Margy whisks me away in the Campion, and we're on our way down the lake.

"No Big 'I' today!" I yell over the roar of the engine.

Margy nods in agreement. The Internet, or Big 'I' as I call it, is often our kiss of death in town. When we crank up our computers, the delays in getting out of the condo are always immense. Nothing is fast for us in cyberspace.

One of today's goals is to stay on schedule as much as possible, so we can make our 2 o'clock estimate for meeting John. It's a complex sequence of events to meet our time goal, but I'd like to be close. If John travels all the way through the Last Chance Trail, I'd like to be as close to on-time as possible. My strategy today is to get as far ahead of schedule as possible, so we can relax and wait for John on the trail above Chippewa Bay.

At the condo, we keep to our promise, only changing into our boots, packing a lunch, and grabbing a forestry map and the GPS. Then we run a few errands in town. By 11:30, we're headed for the airport to hook up to the quad trailer, now only a little behind schedule.

I check in with John by telephone. Since he hasn't left for his trip up the Bunsters to the head of the Last Chance Trail (or even decided

whether the weather is acceptable), I give him a revised meeting time for the trail above Chippewa: 3 o'clock.

"That's fine," he says. "But the weather isn't cooperating."

"We can turn around, even after we get into Theo," I say. "We don't mind getting a little wet."

"Not me," replies John.

He hates pissin'-down rain. Being from California still leaves Margy and me with a sense of excitement at the slightest weather disturbance. Riding in showers isn't a problem for us. A downpour is something else. For now, the sky looks right on the borderline.

"Maybe we'll see you at the top," I say.

"Maybe."

I like indefinite plans, always subject to change with the weather. I've lived a life tied to schedules, phones, email, and commitments. It's satisfying to enter a world wonderfully less structured.

* * * * *

Margy drives her truck out Joyce Ave, towards Highway 101. I chime in with a seemingly unnecessary reminder.

"Don't forget the gas," I say.

"How could we?" she answers.

We could because we have, and we both know it. We normally ride with the luxury of John as our guide, so we tend to simply follow-the-leader. As a leader, John makes sure everything is taken care of, including getting gas for our quads before we leave town. Without him, and our constant complacency under his leadership, we need to think for ourselves. Getting gas would seem to be an obvious function, but once we nearly forgot it when we voyaged out by ourselves.

When we pull into the gas station, our customary lane next to the marine gas aisle is full. So we pause and wait at the entrance. Then Margy wises up, while I continue my John-will-take-care-of-it trance.

"Wait a minute," she says. "The other side of the aisle is open."

We're so used to being with John when we refuel our quads that we have an established sequence. John always pulls into his side of the marine fuel aisle, and we use the other. Without John here today, his side is vacant. So we pull into it and gas up.

We've actually become rather accomplished quad riders in recent months, finally struggling above our pure novice stature under John's on-the-trail instruction. There's little we can't tackle, but venturing out on our own is a mental hurdle.

Leaving the gas station, we drive up Highway 101 to Southview Road, and then north to our favourite (wide!) off-load spot in a section of the main past the Sunshine Coast Trail but well before the stop sign in the wilderness near Larson's Landing.

We off-load efficiently. Who says we can't do this ourselves?

The clouds are now showing more definition. It seems likely this will be a fine day for riding. The recent rain will keep dust to a minimum on the main, an unexpected gift during summer rides. And the temperature is cool, requiring light jackets – perfect riding conditions.

We're only slightly behind schedule. We should be able to make up the time by not making any prolonged side excursions along the way. On the ride back from the cabin tomorrow, we can make all the stops we desire. So meeting John at 3 o'clock still seems realistic – if we don't get lost.

By 1:30, we're headed uphill on the park-like trail into Theodosia. As many times as I've ridden this trail, it's still among my favourites. The forest canopy, lush bushes, and challenging deviations around trees and rocks are a joy on a quad.

Although I ride ahead of Margy through this section, she'll take the lead on most of today's trip. She's still learning to ride her new bike, a Kodiak 450, so I'm not sure of a speed that's comfortable for her. The best solution is to let her set the pace.

We ride with our lights on continually, a procedure providing a measure of safety, as well as a means of communication. On a trip like this, it's possible we won't see another motor vehicle on the trail, but that can result in complacency. When you come around a corner, not expecting traffic, it's best to be seen as easily as possible. Additionally, from behind, I can get Margy's attention by turning off my lights. She keeps track of me in her rear-view mirror, knowing lights-off means I want her to stop.

At the Theo logging dock, we stop for lunch. Then it's a short ride to the Heather Main intersection, where we turn right at the "Y." Our previous trip on this end of Heather Main was in winter, and only a few kilometres up the main to the point where our quads could no longer get traction in the snow. A friend of John's has warned us about the numerous logging spurs that can mislead a rider, particularly an intersection he described in detail. This main is an easy ride, but not well traveled. New spurs can easily lead you astray.

In only a few klicks, the dirt road starts significantly upward. Then we arrive at a split that looks a lot like the intersection we've been cautioned about. Margy stops, and I pull up next to her.

"Is this the spot?" asks Margy, knowing the warning about a split that seems like this one.

"I don't think so," I answer. "It looks like it, but way too early. The road to the right looks like the main to me."

The widest, most significant road bends sharply right and uphill, while a lesser path leads off to the left and downhill. If this is the spot where we're supposed to be careful, we should go left and downhill. My reasoning is that we need to go uphill a long ways before starting down towards Chippewa Bay. We've barely begun, and already we aren't sure of our location. Getting lost on a main isn't a sign of experience.

"I think we should go right," I say. "It looks like the main, and it's uphill. The 'Y' where we go downhill must be quite a bit farther from here."

We discuss the situation some more, noticing the substantial switchback structure on the road climbing to the right. It looks just like I envision Heather Main, climbing significantly onto a high plateau. Of course, we could check our map or the GPS, but we don't. I'm confident this is the right route. Margy agrees, and up we go.

And up and up, winding back and forth on the extensive switchbacks, now into what looks like a new logging area. Meanwhile, I grow less confident this is Heather Main.

Approaching a bridge with some broken boards, Margy comes to a halt. This wooden span looks precarious, and the ravine below is a significant drop. I pull up beside her.

"Maybe we should check the GPS," she says.

Better late than never. The screen of the GPS is difficult to read in the sunshine now glaring through a high overcast. The you-are-here symbol pops up in the middle of nowhere. I try to zoom out, but even at the smallest scale, we appear to be well off the nearest charted road.

"We must be on a road that's too new to appear on the GPS," I say. "That must have been Heather Main back at the intersection."

Down we go, and down and down. By now, we're well behind schedule. There seems little chance we can hit our appointed time for meeting John. Once we're back at the "Y," I'm convinced of our mistake. I turn on my handheld GPS, which shows us firmly back on Heather Main. I show the moving map to Margy.

"If only I'd checked the GPS the first time," I say.

"Must be a guy thing," she replies.

It often is.

Within a few hundred metres after leaving the intersection (for the second time), the downhill path starts decidedly uphill. I notice the place where we parked on our snowshoe trip, and even the spot where I took the cover photo for *Up the Winter Trail*. After passing

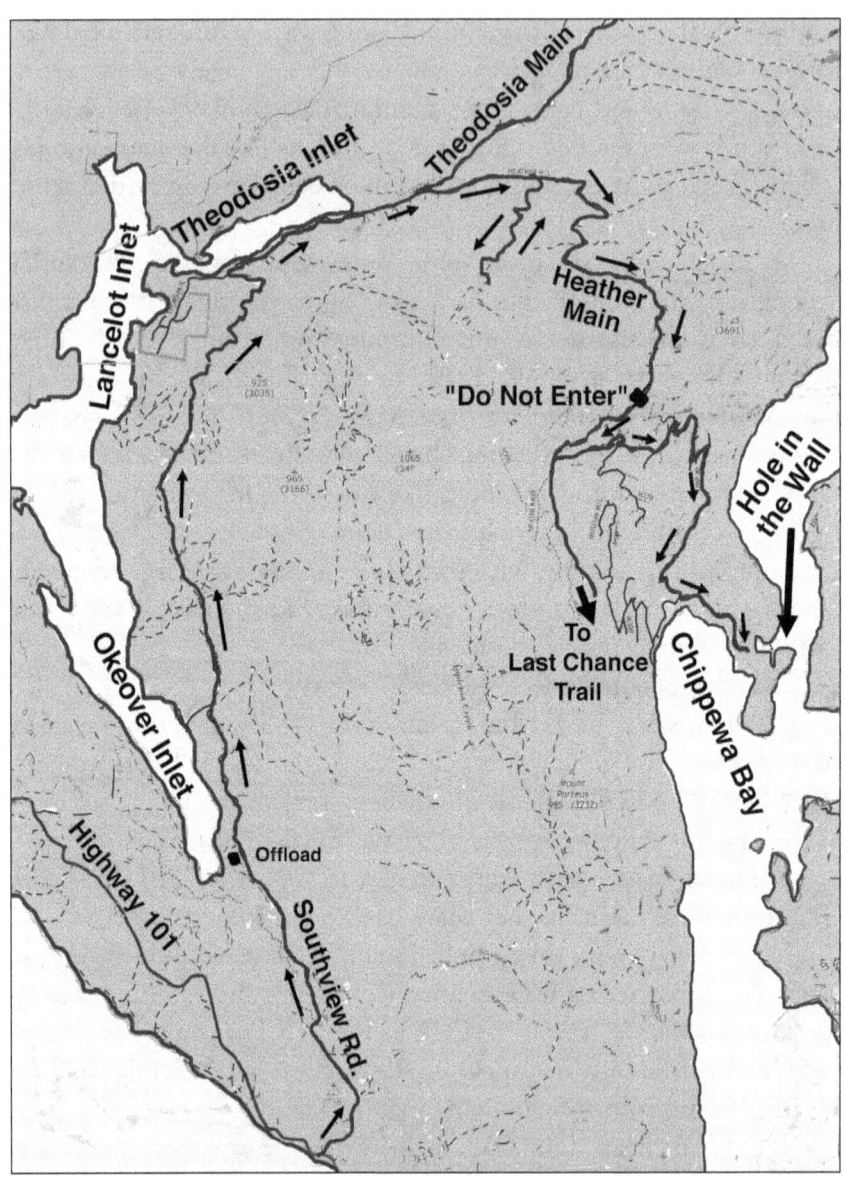

this location, I regret not taking a summer snapshot for comparison. I promise myself I'll stop here for a photo during our trip back down Heather Main tomorrow.

We climb higher, through an old logging area where large second-growth trees form a scenic boundary along the sides of the main. Huge cranes from a previous logging era, now rusted and discarded, sit alongside the road. I'm tempted to stop, and I notice Margy slowing in front of me to investigate. But we continue, sticking to our previous agreement to try to make up for lost time. Tomorrow, on the way back, we'll take the opportunity to look over this old equipment.

Blow-downs haven't stopped us yet, although several small logs cross the main. Large logs, previously cut by another quad rider or logger, give us a wide enough swath to navigate. But now there is a good-sized log in front of us, completely across the road. Margy stops and looks back over her shoulder as I pull up behind her.

"Give it a try," I suggest, knowing I can crank my chainsaw, if necessary.

She pulls forward and easily crawls over the log with her front wheels. But when she tries to pull over with her rear tires, she spins to a stop. When she looks back, I raise my arm, with four fingers outstretched. She nods, and I watch her reach with her right hand to shift into four-wheel drive. Her new bike has the added convenience she wasn't used to on her smaller two-wheel drive model. It's her first chance to use it when it's really needed.

This time, Margy maneuvers her rear wheels over the log with little problem. I shift into four-wheel drive, pull into position behind her, and get over the log on my first try.

I pull up next to Margy, and suggest she use special caution now for opposite-direction traffic. I'm not certain where we are, but we could be coming close to the place where we'll meet John. With our helmets on, we'll never hear John approaching over the noise of our motors.

We drive another klick, Margy still in front, when suddenly the road is completely blocked at an intersection where a spur comes in from the left. There's no doubt which road is Heather Main, but the entire intersection is blocked in an unusual way.

A fallen fir tree, with a plethora of thick branches, covers all but the edge of Heather Main. From the end of the tree, a rope is stretched across the small spur with a blue-on-white sign that reads *Do Not Enter*.

Margy slows, and I expect her to stop, but she doesn't. Instead, she maneuvers towards the edge of the main where a small gap between the tree and the ditch allows her to pass. She scrunches low in her seat and drives cautiously under the branches, with just enough clearance for a quad and a hunched rider. I'm amazed she doesn't stop to discuss her decision. But I drop low in my seat and follow her path, getting whacked in the helmet and arms by thick branches.

On the other side, Margy accelerates again. I'm sure we're still on Heather Main, but my thoughts return to the unusual intersection, the fallen tree, and that sign. I add throttle to catch up to her. Although we are now safely clear of the fallen tree, what was that sign all about? Blue-on-white, not red or yellow, and no indication of what the warning might be. Simply: *Do Not Enter*. A blue-on-white sign doesn't seem to imply danger, but could this be a road blasting area?

As I ride on, I can't let go of the mystery. The main is wide and comfortable. On the other hand, a blast of dynamite could certainly ruin our day. Yet, Margy didn't seem to even hesitate back there, which isn't like her, so she must feel comfortable with this. So should I.

As we drive farther, the view down to Powell Lake is majestic. But it also bodes concern. I easily identify Chippewa Bay, Cassiar Island, and Inland Lake, so we are obviously moving far south. But farther south than I expected. It seems we are already past where we should start down towards Chippewa Bay. And directly ahead of us are the looming Bunsters, closer than I expected. Maybe we're now off Heather Main, headed towards the Last Chance Trail.

A "Y" ahead brings us to a stop. Neither path is very wide. The trail to the left goes steeply down, and the one to the right seems headed uphill and straight for the Bunsters.

"Do you think we've gone too far?" I ask. "We're way south of Chippewa."

"Maybe," replies Margy. "The turnoff to Chippewa might have been the intersection with the fallen tree and the sign."

"What about the sign?" I ask. "Didn't it seem weird to you?"

"Well, yes, but I thought the sign applied to the spur that came in from the left. The gap in that fallen tree seemed the logical place to go."

We sit with our engines off, talking quietly about our options. Finally, we decide we've gone too far, so we'll head back to the intersection behind us. Just when I'm about to start my engine, I hear a motor in the distance.

"John!" I say. "Do you hear him?"

"Sounds like a quad," says Margy. "Back where the intersection was blocked."

The motor noise draws nearer. Then two quads round the bend. Bro is barking his fool head off. John's friend, Doug, is in the other quad. They're all laughing (barking too).

"Didn't you see the sign?" yells Doug, as he comes to a halt next to us.

"Oh!" I yell, as John turns off his engine.

Now it all comes into focus. Of course, the blue-and-white sign wasn't your normal logging road sign, because John and Doug created it. And the rope and fallen tree were out of place too. Because they were placed there by them.

"You just blew on through," says John, with a sense of disappointment. "We expected you to stop and try to figure it out. We wanted to watch you hack away at the tree with your saw."

"But you got there too soon," says Doug. "We weren't finished yet. Did you see the blasting caps?"

"Blasting caps?" I say. "No, Margy led me past the tree and the sign too fast."

"We were going to pretend to blow up the little reservoir near the intersection by lobbing rocks into the water," says Doug. "But we didn't have time to get things set up before you arrived."

Yes, that would have gotten our attention.

* * * * *

We start down the trail to Chippewa, which begins right at the "Y" where we stopped. A huge switchback leads us down from well south of First Narrows all the way back to Elvis Rock in the north. The enormous switchback explains why we felt so far south – because we were!

John leads our four-vehicle procession, followed by Doug, and then Margy, then me. The switchback deviates far to the north, descending through a slash towards the highest point we were able to reach on snowshoes last winter during our climb up from Chippewa Bay. On that hike, the deepening snow and our deteriorating level of energy stopped us. At the time, we were well above the altitude where a vehicle could drive in winter. The upper reaches of Heather Main hide for months under an amazing burden of snow. (To my amazement, the following winter, John takes his quad through the entire stretch of upper Heather Main, riding on top of a heavy crust of snow – a feat I thought was impossible.)

I recognize the spot where we were stopped on a snowshoe climb the previous year, and pause to take a photo. In my mind, I compare this summer vista to the winter view that I remember at this same spot.

From here, the descent down to Chippewa Bay is easy to navigate, dropping though stunning groves of trees interspersed with invasive logging slashes where huge piles of wood scraps are stacked on the side of the road. We continue down the switchback far to the north of First Narrows, with a majestic view looking south towards Hole in the Wall.

When most of the descent is behind us, John and Doug turn back uphill, to ride back through the Last Chance Trail, while we continue farther down until we are looking directly down on the cabins in the Hole. We park along the overgrown logging road, and then wind down the narrow path to the tin boat that awiats us for the short ride back to our cabin. We have returned to the tranquil setting of our floating cabin on Powell Lake.

* * * * *

The next morning dawns nearly cloudless. We eat a leisurely breakfast, then motor back into the Hole in the tin boat. We climb back up the trail to where our quads are parked, and get ready to ride.

Once out on the logging road that winds along Chippewa Bay, we're on our way in standard riding mode – lights on, Margy in the lead. The weather is even better than yesterday, with the sun already shining strong. With the air warmer now, we ride in long-sleeve shirts without jackets. Our rain pants, donned yesterday just-in-case, sit in our aft quad boxes.

We pass the hiking path to Chippewa Bay that leads to one of John's favourite warm-water swimming spots. Then we make a sharp right turn, rather than left to the logging dock, to head up the northbound side of the long switchback. Before turning southbound in the lengthy climb, we pause at a majestic overlook of Powell Lake, where glaciated peaks spread northward. I get off my quad and walk over to Margy, who is still sitting astride her bike. It's a great spot to take in the view of the lake below.

"Have you checked your gas?" says Margy.

"Not lately, but I'm sure we have plenty," I reply.

I walk back to my bike to check the gas gauge. The needle rests slightly below half, but we are on a moderate upward slope, where a fuel indicator might be inaccurate. Besides, like airplanes, its best not to rely on gas gauges. It's better to depend on the odometer (or flight time in an airplane) for more accurate fuel reserves.

"My gauge has been showing below half for the past few klicks," notes Margy.

"But it's been mostly uphill. My trip metre shows only 61 klicks since off-loading yesterday."

"And it's less distance on the way back, because of our unexpected logging spur excursion yesterday," says Margy.

"Yes, getting lost added on quite a few klicks."

Oops – I said the wrong word. We weren't really "lost," just momentarily unsure of our location.

"So how far can we go on a full tank?" asks Margy.

We seldom stretch our fuel to the limit, primarily because long rides like this are unusual for us. This trip is the first time we've gone two days in a row without refueling. The truth is, I really don't know how far we can ride on a full tank.

"Easily over a 100 kilometres, not including our reserve."

I say this with confidence, but my actual knowledge is limited. I remember riding once more than 100 klicks, and twice I've switched to *Reserve*. But then, I was riding with John. As usual, I relied on him to make sure I didn't travel beyond my gas limit. John can mentally compute fuel range on a quad within a few kilometres, and would never let me ride to fuel exhaustion. Today, however, it's up to us.

"I guess we should've topped off at the cabin, just in case," says Margy.

She's right – we could have easily added gas when we spent the night at our cabin. I always have extra fuel stored there. But when we finished our ride yesterday, I didn't even glance at my gas gauge. It just seemed obvious we had plenty for the return trip.

"Should have," I agree. "But we're still in good shape. It can't be over 40 kilometres back to the truck from here, so that totals 100. Well less than our range, especially when you add in the reserve."

"So how far on reserve?" she asks.

"At least 20 klicks," I state, with conviction.

"Maybe we should hold off the side excursions, just in case," she says.

"Good idea. Let's see how our gas gauges look on the level, and we'll head straight back. By the time we get to Theo, we'll have a better idea of our situation. If we haven't gone onto reserve by then, we'll easily make it back to the truck."

This isn't life-or-death. Instead, it's merely amateurs in action. We obviously should have refueled at the cabin. And I regret I'm not more knowledgeable about our fuel range.

"What about these gauges?" Margy asks. "Do they hit zero when our regular tank is dry, or when our reserve runs out?"

"Good question."

But I don't know the answer. I do know our reserve fuel isn't in a separate tank. I remember running out of fuel near Haslam Lake with John, the engine sputtering to a stop. Then I switched to *Reserve* for the short distance back to our trucks. Same fuel tank – just a valve to switch from the normal standpipe to a lower outlet in the tank. In reality, the reserve feature is merely a warning you need to find gas soon.

"I'm not sure," I admit. "I think the gauge reads empty when the regular fuel runs out. But our odometer gives a better indication of our fuel than those funky gauges."

The worst that could happen is we run out of fuel near our truck, after climbing out of Theodosia. We should be able to flag down someone (if there is someone), since nobody around here would pass someone in trouble. Or we could walk the remaining distance to the truck. It's more of an inconvenience than a major problem.

We climb the remaining portion of the switchback, heading back south for several kilometres, then finally north again on a fairly flat stretch of Heather Main. On the level road, my gas gauge still indicates below the half mark.

At the first old crane, parked beside the road, we pull off to explore the machinery. The rusted behemoth is an abandoned monument to an era now past. On Heather Main, logging activity is minimal these days, at least on this end of the road. But old derelict logging equipment was left where it was last used, museum-like specimens of technology now many decades old. The large crane arm supports a big pulley and cables driven by mechanical levers without hydraulic assistance, evidence of equipment long extinct.

We climb around to the back of the rusting skeleton, looking for a date of production. Usually, these old machines have a proudly molded date in a prominent location. We find no date stamp, but this crane must be at least 50 years old.

While we're stopped, I use the opportunity to try to phone John or Rick from atop this high plateau. These days, cell phone coverage, even in remote sections of coastal BC, is quite good. It has to be that way for logging companies to conduct their business effectively.

John isn't home, but Rick may be in his taxicab, so I dial his number. When he answers, I ask about the range of our quads.

"Margy and I are up on Heather Main, and we need some specs on a Kodiak 450," I say. "Do you know any local experts?"

"Might," Rick replies.

Rick is an expert on almost any vehicle, land or sea. Regarding quads, he knows just about everything.

"What's the fuel range of our bikes?" I ask. "We've driven about 70 klicks, and we've got 30 to go."

"No problem," replies Rick. "You've got at least 100 before you hit reserve. And then you can count on about another 30. That's in fairly flat conditions for a bike that's well broken in."

Rick knows our route, and it's not flat. He also knows Margy's bike is nearly brand-new, not yet fully broken in.

"Our gauges show we might be getting in trouble," I add.

"Those gauges are crap," says Rick. "Don't even pay attention to them."

After talking to Rick, I feel a lot more confident about our situation. Still, it would be best to avoid side excursions today, at least until we're back in Theodosia Valley, where there are usually a few people and we're closer to our truck.

Our next stop is at the intersection where John and Doug set up the "Do Not Enter" trap yesterday. The intersection is now clear, but the remnants of the tree they moved into the road and the old blasting caps are off to the side. I find the blue-and-white warning sign in the ditch. I put the sign back on the tree for a photo, then I strap it onto my quad. Somewhere, sometime, I'll find an opportunity to return this sign to John and Doug at a place and time they least expect.

The rest of the ride is a breeze, mostly downhill and without incident. We come to the spot on the east end of Heather Main where we hiked on snowshoes, and I turn off my headlights to ask Margy to stop.

Sitting astride my quad at this site, I reflect on how radically different this spot is now, compared to winter. It's beautiful in both seasons, but an entirely different place.

Farther down the main, we enter a logging equipment area where several vehicles are parked. We pass below a swooping helicopter that has just taken off from a grass pad near the road. Then we travel a few hundred metres south on Theodosia Main to the entrance to Rupert's Farm.

Summer on Heather Main (top) compared to winter photo (from cover of *Up the Winter Trail)* at the same location.

On the trail into the farm, we stop at a spot on the bank of the Theodosia River where salmon run during the spawning season. We're still a few days (or weeks) early, and the stream burbles contently and empty of the big fish that will soon crowd these shallow waters. We eat our lunch, and Margy switches to her reserve fuel, concerned about losing her engine during the climb-out from Theodosia. I leave my bike's fuel valve on the main tank, hoping to determine the odometer distance for fuel depletion of a Kodiak 450.

Leaving Rupert's Farm, we motor down the main to a turnoff near the mudflats at Theodosia Inlet. The tide is low, and the meandering river delta to the north forms a foreground for mountains rising high into the backcountry.

From here, it's a relaxing climb up from the logging dock, back down the ridge, and out of Theodosia Valley. On the final stretch of road, headed back to our truck, I run my main fuel tank dry. I coast to a stop on the shoulder, switch to *Reserve*, and restart my quad. My kilometre trip metre reads 100.9. Before I pull out onto the main again, I add an out-loud comment to myself that seems appropriate: "Right on, Rick!"

◊ ◊ ◊ ◊ ◊ ◊

Chapter 8

Khartoum

Before the Scanlon Dam was built at the south end of Lois Lake, there were three lakes: Gordon Pasha, Upper Pasha (Second Lake), and Khartoum (Third Lake). With the flooding of the lower portion, the two Pashas were renamed Lois Lake. Khartoum Lake (still called "Third Lake" by those who remember the Gordon Pasha Lakes) is connected to Lois by a winding river. The popular ATV route to Khartoum follows Stillwater Main to the fish farm on the north side of Lois Lake, then along Khartoum Main (Third Lake Main).

At the head of Khartoum Lake, John and Rick have cleared the trail leading to the inlet. Today, on a mid-April day with a forecast high of 12 degrees, Margy and I plan to explore the area, and maybe even join John and Rick as they continue to work on reopening another trail on the upper reaches of Third Lake Main, connecting to the Good Hope Trail. So far, John and Rick have cut back the alder branches on only a short stretch of the road, their progress hampered by the deep snow that still remains from winter.

Margy and I get an early start, since I hate to keep John waiting. We aren't planning to ride with John and Rick all the way to the alder pruning area, but we should be able to keep up with them as far as the head of Khartoum Lake.

At the hangar, we hook up the quad trailer and pull to a stop outside the airport gate, where I telephone John. I seldom call him before 9 o'clock, since I don't want to wake him up. But I also don't want to delay his departure this morning. Of course, I shouldn't worry about it, since John doesn't wait for anyone.

"He already left," says Rick, when I phone at 9:10. "I'm about to leave, too."

"That can only mean one thing," I say. "You're gonna have a long day."

When John leaves this early, he's concerned about making it back before dark. Twilight will extend after 8 o'clock, so it'll be a long day.

"We've got a lot of work to do," says Rick.

"Can you give me some directions to the trail down to the head of Khartoum?" I ask. "I've never been past the campground."

"It's easy to find. When you get a ways up the lake, there's a road that splits off to your right. You can see the lake from the intersection. Go past that road and take the next right turn you find. It turns into a quad trail right away, and takes you all the way to the river."

"Thanks," I say. "You'd better get going without us. We've got to get gas, and everything takes us forever, you know."

"I know," says Rick.

Margy and I are famous for taking our time, at least in comparison to Rick and John.

* * * * *

At the gas station on Highway 101, we pump gas into Margy's truck. When traveling with John, we always use the marine gas pumps for our quads. After all, it's a few cents cheaper and probably better for our engines. But the marine pumps are at another gas island, so it's tempting to use regular gas for both the truck and quads today.

"John wouldn't like it if he knew, but let's fill up our bikes here."

"You'll get caught," says Margy.

"John's already left, so we won't get caught."

Getting caught by John isn't dangerous, but it can be unsettling. And he always catches me, no matter where or when.

Just as we finish fueling the truck, Rick pulls in with his pickup truck and quad in back. He doesn't need gas, but wants to make sure we find a good spot to off-load.

"Goat Main is a mess," he says. "Lots of potholes, but you can park at the chipper at the bottom of Lois. You'll see my truck there. Lots of space."

Rick thinks I know where everything is. Of course, I don't. I nod my head, but I'm not even sure what a chipper looks like.

When he leaves, Margy reminds me: "You got caught."

"Almost," I reply.

Although Rick has now left, in deference to John (and Rick), we pull forward and fill up our quads with marine gas. And we save a total of 30 cents.

* * * * *

On Goat Main, we pass a good turnout that would easily hold our truck and double-quad trailer. But Rick may be waiting for us at the chipper, so we keep driving.

In another 100 metres, we turn down the short *Do Not Enter* route to the lower road. It's safe, since we can see all the way to the bottom, and nothing is coming. Rick's truck and his green quad next to it are visible through the trees. Rick is already aboard his bike, helmet on, and ready to ride.

We barely start down the one-way road when Rick pulls up next to us, riding his Grizzly. We stop to talk, which means we are idling the wrong way on a one-way hill, now completely blocking it, which makes me nervous.

"You can pull up right next to my truck," yells Rick over the sound of his motor. "There's lots of room for your trailer."

"Okay. Where's John."

"He's gone farther up the main to Tin Hat Junction. That makes it easier on Bro for long quad rides like this."

Rick roars off, and we creep the rest of the way down the wrong-way road towards his truck. This parking area is Rick's idea of lots of room, not ours. Margy prefers plenty of space to maneuver, and this isn't such a place. Besides, the dirt looks soft.

"We can go back to the last wide turnoff," I suggest.

"I'd prefer that," replies Margy.

She makes a wide swing into the chipper parking lot on the other side of the road, which is a lot wider. So that's what a chipper looks like?

Margy drives back up the one-way road (the right way this time), and onto Goat Main, headed back in the direction we came from. She pulls off into the wide turnout, a fine spot to off-load our quads.

While I back my quad down the ramp, an old yellow (now mostly scruffy black) school bus passes by, headed north. Old buses like this get an extended life when they're used as recreational vehicles. But in the damp forest, they don't keep their shiny paint for long.

Soon we're ready to ride. We head up Goat Main to the turnout that looks up the full extent of Lois Lake. We pull off the road for a moment to absorb the beauty of the view.

We pass John's parked truck at Tin Hat Junction, and turn right towards Khartoum Lake. As soon as we come around the corner, I notice the old school bus in front of us, driving slow over the rough road. The driver sees us in his rearview mirror and immediately pulls over to the shoulder to let us pass. Quads can make good time on rough roads, overtaking even smooth-riding vehicles (which this bus isn't). I wave as we go by, and the driver thrusts his hand out the window in a V-sign: Peace, man – sixties style.

We stop briefly at the sign forest marking the intersection to so many wonderful places in this region: Freda Mountain, the Knuckleheads, Mount Diadem, Horseshoe Lake.

Just before crossing the bridge where Freda Creek pours into Lois Lake, I lead us off into the pull-out. A camper-van is parked a bit

farther in, enjoying a scenic spot on this mid-April day full of sunny breaks. The water below looks perfect for trout.

We get off our quads, and I dig into my daypack for fishing gear.

"I don't think I have a fishing pole," I say to Margy. "Can't find one in my pack."

I dig around, looking for my collapsible pole. Since there's none here, it means there are two back in the truck. I removed them from my bag when fishing season ended, and now spring fishing has arrived without a pole.

We drive across the bridge and continue on Khartoum Main (Third Lake Main). Margy leads now as we pass the fish farm, and enter an area where a wide slash shows lots of activity for a Saturday. Besides the big yellow crane on the road high above, there are numerous orange crew-cab pickup trucks parked along the main. A large sign reads: *Caution: Blasting Area.*

We overtake an orange pickup that comes to a halt in front of us – not to block our passage, but to talk to us instead. Since Margy is

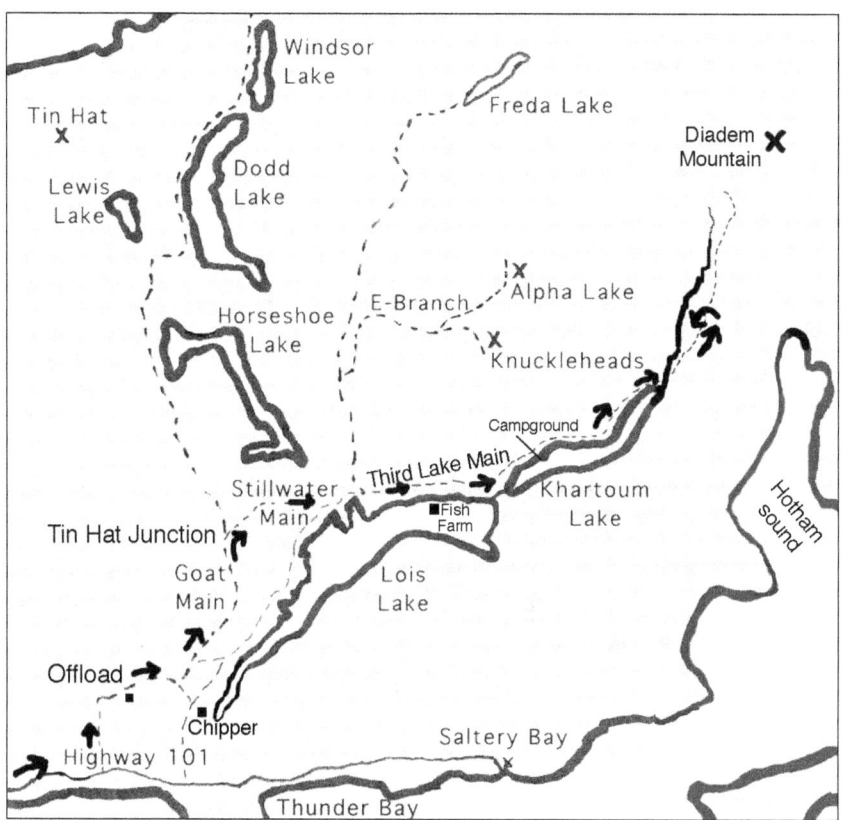

first in line, I pull up behind her and watch as she discusses something with the young man who has stepped out of his cab. Over the noise of our engines, I can't hear what he's saying, but in few minutes, I see him wave us around his truck. When we stop at a turnout farther up the road, I ask Margy what the driver said.

"They're blasting on the road up above," says Margy. "He wanted to make sure we stayed on the mainline, because there's lots of road work here today."

"That's strange for a Saturday," I reply. "Logging must be doing better than I thought."

But it isn't, and everyone knows it. The escalating Canadian loonie is killing lumber exports to the States. Softwood exports have always been a sore spot for Canada, and the nearly-on-par dollar has made matters even worse. Yet they are building logging roads here on a Saturday.

Both road builders and robins are everywhere. The robins are a cheery sign of spring, flittering across the road and resting on branches overlooking the main.

Within another kilometre, another truck is stopped and waiting for us. The large John Deere dump-truck-style vehicle is painted bright red. At first I think it's an emergency vehicle, but there are no such markings. The driver is standing in the center of the road in a bright orange vest, waving both arms at us. I'm suddenly uncomfortable, wondering whether we're going to be asked to turn back.

"What model is that?" yells the smiling man, as we come to a stop. "I need to know which quad I should buy!"

The jovial fellow with a blond mustache is from Penticton, recently moved here as a new employee of Plutonic Power. He's all enthused about buying a quad.

"So it isn't logging we see today," I say. "You're building power lines."

"All the way to Goat Lake, then on up to Toba Inlet," bellows the man. "Building roads for the transmission lines. Lots of work for people like me."

"Quite a project," says Margy. "I've been reading about it."

"Run-of-river electrical power," says the orange-vested man. "Logging is in bad shape, which is why I've moved here. Those logging companies are just too used to doing things the American way."

It's the kind of statement that always gives me a good internal laugh. Surely he doesn't know I'm an American, but it puts a smile on my face.

We talk about quads for quite a while. Meanwhile, our vehicles completely block the road. But there's nobody else in sight.

"This quad is a good size," recommends Margy. "Easy to maneuver, but plenty of power for almost anything."

"I'll find me a quad, and then a woman who likes the outdoors," chirps the man. "You got a sister?"

"She's one of a kind," I interrupt. "I'm lucky I found her."
Now that's an understatement.

* * * * *

Margy makes the turn down to the campground at Khartoum Lake, and I follow. We pull into the campsite where we spent the night during a kayak trip up Lois Lake, through the winding river, and into Khartoum. This campground is one of our favourites, and the place we chose to hold the book launch hotdog roast for the original *Up the Main*. On a rainy November day, twenty members of the Powell River ATV Club (and other friends) joined me in celebration of the new book. This is as far up Khartoum Lake as we've been so far. But from here, we can see up north to the head we are about to visit.

Back on Third Lake Main, we enter an area where alder branches lie alongside the road, freshly pruned. This is obviously the work of John and Rick, and it goes on for several kilometres. We pass the first road to the right (which Rick has warned us not to take) and then reach the entrance to the trail to the head.

When we pull off the main, Margy stops. I maneuver around her and lead the way across a small stream easily forded on our quads. The trail is a wonderful surprise, even more scenic than expected. It's a twisted path winding through a forest of thin-trunked trees carpeted with a mixture of brilliant spring-green moss and ferns.

Huge old-growth stumps line sections of the trail, lending a historic perspective to the lush forest. Portions of the trail are challenging, including a turn with a mix of fallen logs and gravelly soil.

After maneuvering through this corner, I stop and watch in my rearview mirror, waiting for Margy to appear. She's delayed, so I get off my bike and walk back to find her. Her quad sits at an awkward angle, tilted upward on the left side where she has stopped in the middle of the turn.

"It's too tipsy," says Margy, holding on tight to her handlebars.

"You shouldn't stop on a corner like this," I say. "It makes it feel even more unstable."

"But it's so tilted," she says in a whining voice.

"Get over it!" I yell.

Margy knows I'm only kidding. Using these words, John has coaxed her through her bout with quad "acrophobia" (*Up the Main*, Chapter 10). John's "gentle" coercion helped more than it hurt, so he still uses it when Margy backs off in difficult terrain like this.

I provide some counterbalance weight on the high side of Margy's Kodiak, and without any further difficulties, she makes it through the tough spot. Then the trail opens onto the rocky bank of the Lois River, a beautiful roaring stream at the inlet to Khartoum Lake.

"Perfect fishing, I bet," I say. "Too bad there's no fishing pole."

"Look at these rocks!" marvels Margy.

We love rocks, and these are gorgeous. Geologically, they tell a story we don't entirely understand. But the stones are beautiful water-worn granite, quartz, with various stratified and diked minerals. We collect a few colourful specimens to take home.

Looking north, Mount Diadem stands tall and stark with snow along its flanks. It could be the Matterhorn, but this isn't Switzerland.

We eat our lunch on the boulder-strewn shore, swatting at our first major mosquito attack of spring. The scenery far overshadows the bugs.

* * * * *

Back on the mainline, we travel up towards the Good Hope Trail, where Rick and John are working. Their pruning efforts are evident all along the way, and it makes travel easy for us.

Snow appears along the side of the road, then thicker drifts begin to cover sections of the trail. Quad tread marks lead on through the white patches.

We catch up with John and Rick sooner than expected. They are making slower progress than they hoped. And in only a few hundred more metres they'll be completely stopped by the snow, until the spring melt allows them to continue. Eventually, their work will reconnect Third Lake Main with the Good Hope Trail.

I take my pruning shears from my quad box, and pitch in to help. Margy doesn't have any shears today, so she lingers behind as we work at the overhanging branches. I clip along the sides of the road for only a half-hour, but John and Rick appreciate the effort.

"We won't be able to get much farther today," says John. "Too much snow up ahead."

"Margy and I are going to head back down," I say. "Someday I'll ride on the Good Hope Trail."

"Not for a few months," laughs John. "But we'll get it ready for you."

I walk back to our bikes, where I find Margy sitting on her quad reading a book about polar exploration.

"Looks cold," I say, motioning to her book.

"This book or up ahead?" she quips.

"Both," I reply. "Let's go home."

It's fun to think about going home. Especially when home is here.

Chapter 9

Granite Lake 6

The windshield of Margy's truck, parked in the Westview Marina lot, is covered with ice. We'll soon be even further behind schedule.

As Margy starts the engine and cranks up the defroster, I look for the ice scraper. In the back seat, my rain gear and gloves are spread out, an attempt to dry them after our previous quad ride. For three days the wet clothes have done little more than steam up the truck's interior, making the windshield and dashboard a soggy, wet mess mixed with icy patches. Fortunately, on this cold but clear November morning, we won't need rain gear for our ride. Warm and dry clothes will be needed instead.

I locate the scraper in the back pocket of the passenger seat and attack the outside of the windshield, while the City Motors tow truck hooks up to a derelict pickup without a parking permit a few spaces away. I recognize Bob, the smiling driver, who is a one-man show when it comes to retrieving vehicles all over town. A tow-away in the marina today probably means the truck is more than a few days over the limit.

From over my shoulder, a squirt of fluid hits the windshield. When I look up, Bob is pointing a can of de-icing fluid at the glass, spraying away what would've taken me a lot of time and effort.

"Will this help?" he says, smiling away.

I hope so, because he's already spraying up a storm.

"Man, that sure does the trick," I respond. "Thanks!"

"Sure. Want me to hit the inside?"

"No, that's just fine. Put it on his bill," I say.

Bob laughs, walks away, and Margy and I get out of the parking lot fast enough to put us nearly back on schedule.

* * * * *

"We're always running behind," I say to Margy as she maneuvers the truck around the sharp corner in the drive-through lane.

"Makes for too much fast food," she replies. "Maybe we should try leaving earlier next time."

"You mean that would solve it?"

It's difficult to meet John's demanding be-there-at-nine schedule. Lots of errands in town accumulate while we're up the lake. Typically, they take longer than expected, and pretty soon we exceed our optimistic time projections. This morning, we'll cram in a visit to Canadian Tire, the post office, and a breakfast drive-through. We've budgeted an extra hour, which doesn't seem nearly enough until we realize we can skip the post office since it isn't open this early anyway. But our timeline must include a trip to the airport to hook up the quad trailer, a process that takes a realistic twenty minutes from the moment we enter the gate.

By the time we get back from our quad ride, stores will be closed, and we'll have to put off more errands until our next visit to town. So we perpetually get further behind and try to shove as much as possible into another be-there-at-nine morning. But today we somehow manage to pull into John's five minutes ahead of time, and that makes us all happy.

* * * * *

After gassing up three quads and two trucks, I ride with John and Bro while Margy follows in her truck, pulling our quad trailer. We use our normal route through Cranberry, then along Haslam and Duck Lakes towards one of our favourite off-load spots near Mud Lake. When we pull into the turnout, Terry's already there, sitting on his quad and ready to ride. Margy has fallen well behind as the victim of a bouncy trailer on a rough dirt road.

Eldon pulls in right behind us, but maneuvers his pickup truck to the other side of the road, where he quickly off-loads his quad. If you're looking for speed, it's Eldon.

"I passed Margy back there," he says. "She's having a bit of a time with those pot holes."

"You've got her spot," I say. "But maybe she can make the turn."

"Lots of room over here," replies Eldon. "Of course, she does need lots of room."

Kid as we may, Margy maneuvers her truck increasingly well with the long trailer. Backing up is still not her specialty, but she manages to get into confined spots – eventually.

I hear Margy approaching, so I go out into the center of the road to signal for her to swing around to the right and park behind Eldon.

"Clear the area!" I yell to Eldon.

"Yuh, right," he yells back.

Margy swings her truck through a complete course reversal, ending near the perfect spot for off-loading. I motion for her to pull forward just a bit to straighten the trailer, then hold up my hand: *Stop*.

I look over at John, who is nodding his head in appreciation of the parking exercise, and then I glance at Eldon. His forehead is crinkled in a sign of applause: "I'm impressed!" he yells.

Now for the agonizing part. Off-loading while people are waiting for us is always a demanding experience. Terry was ready when we arrived, and John and Eldon are speed demons. Margy and I, on the other hand, are as slow as molasses. In our defense, it takes longer to unstrap two quads and back them off a trailer, we don more clothes (almost always too many for the conditions), and we tend to haul more stuff than we could possibly need. In short, we are amateurs compared to these guys.

Today everyone is patient with us, even John. Besides, he's having a heck of a time trying to get Bro ready to ride. It's a cold day, so Bro is dressed in his sweater and blue outer rain jacket, but his head is unprotected. John brought a scarf for him and is trying to wrap it around Bro's head. Bro doesn't take too kindly to anything covering his ears. He ends up looking like a dog in a granny suit, trying to avoid my camera.

Today's hat design is a failure and will be shed by Bro later in the ride. As the winter progresses, John won't give up. He repeatedly tries new designs to protect Bro's head until he eventually (in later chapters of this book) finds a version that works.

"Are you guys finally ready?" I ask, as I struggle with my gloves, trying to place a heavy pair over a thinner set.

John, Eldon, and Terry have been over by John's truck, talking about quad axles and transmissions for the past ten minutes. Margy is on her bike and ready to ride. I'm the slow poke, per usual.

"I guess we're finally ready," says John.

The three guys hop on their quads, start them up, and are gone before I can finish adjusting my gloves. Margy waits for me, then pulls out of the turnout. I bring up the rear.

John leads us east to the Y-junction, where we turn to the right on Branch 3. When we come to the sign for Granite Lake Main, we enter the trail towards the lake I'm familiar with, but almost immediately deviate to the right, entering an unmarked spur John calls Granite Lake 6. This is an old logging road we expect to be impassible near our destination, a snowy place called Walt Hill or simply "Radio Hill," where a logging repeater antenna sits. We know we won't be able to make it all the way up to the tower, but an older antenna (partly dismantled) sits lower on the hill, next to a cabin and scenic overlook on the Sunshine Coast Trail. We hope to make it that far today.

Even before we get to the cabin, we expect to encounter alders that will thwart us. John carries his trusty chainsaw, and Eldon, Terry, and I have pruning shears to assist. All of our efforts will be needed to drag the scrub alders clear of the trail, so this isn't expected to be a ride in the park.

The lower portion of Granite Lake 6 is in fine shape, with a few rocky sections where four-wheel drive nudges us through. Patches of snow begin to appear, indicating the higher elevations will be more difficult, with drifts on the trail and snow-laden branches overhead. Typically, trailside alders can be battled by the first rider, who pulls down on the snowy branches and lets them spring upward and outward, throwing off their load. The first rider is John, so he and Bro can expect a cold dousing.

Conditions are better than expected. The snow deepens as we climb, and we must stop occasionally to cut through the alders. But most of the time, John simply pulls down on the overhanging branches to clear the path for the rest of us. He and Bro take the brunt of the battle. Maybe Bro is glad he's wearing his scarf after all.

Hikers have been through here in recent weeks, clearing the trail, and that makes our travel easier. John has never ridden this high on Granite 6, although he has hiked it all the way to the cabin. It's possible we are the first quads that have climbed this high up the old logging road this season.

We stop at a spot where the trail rounds a series of ponds covered with ice and a thin layer of snow. Since we're anxious to make it to the cabin, we hike off the road only far enough to get a quick look at the tranquil scene.

"We can stop on the way back down," says John. "There's at least one more pond back in there."

"I used to come up here all the time in my truck," says Eldon. "That was years ago, when the road was clear. Haven't been here in years though."

Two very experienced mountain riders, John and Eldon, are excited by today's route. There aren't many places they haven't visited in this region. They've both been here before, but not in a long time. And never on quads.

Terry, a novice to quad riding, has spent decades hiking this area. But now he drives a big Grizzly 700, with independent suspension and power steering. In comparison to his hiking experience, he must consider this child's play, which in many ways it is.

Margy and I, as always, are overwhelmed wherever we go. The majestic scenery never seems to end. Add a little snow to the mix, and it's a winter wonderland.

After leaving the ponds, we follow a winding trail that clings to the side of the mountain, with a significant drop-off to one side. The first rider (John) has the most work to do, occasionally bogging down in the snow and then finally thrusting through. He must exercise care on the narrow sloped sections of the trail. Not only is it a steep drop-off, his tracks define our route to the top. If his tracks aren't perfect, neither are we.

At one spot, Margy gets a little too far to the downhill side and comes to a halt, precariously perched on the edge. I can imagine her concern, not just because of her perilous position, but because she continually battles what I call quad "acrophobia," fear of steep slopes. I stop my quad and run ahead to assist.

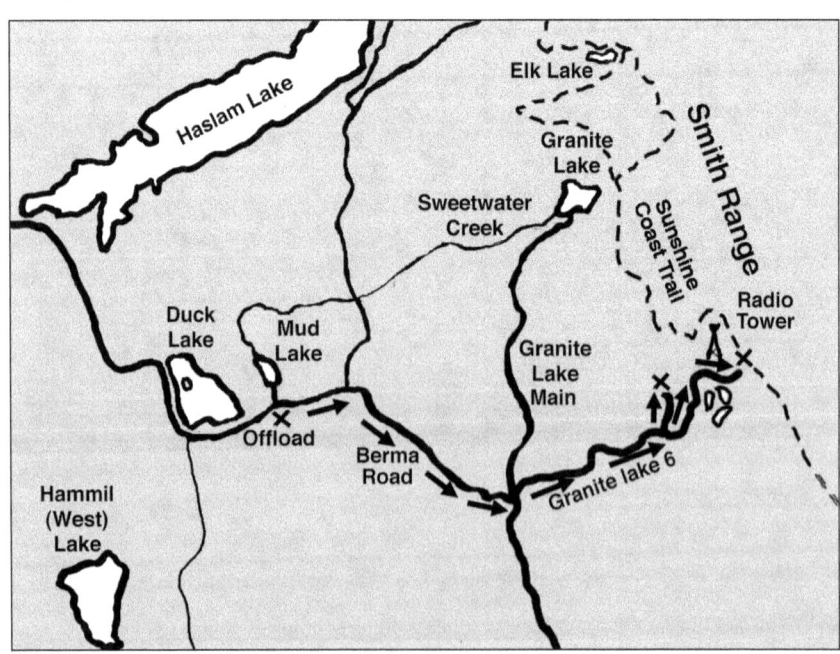

"I'm okay," she says, as I step between her quad and the drop-off.

I know Margy, and I know she feels better when she can't see the downhill slope. I look through her goggles, into her eyes, and I can tell there is a tinge of panic.

I stand on a small shelf where it's safe for me to help block her downhill view and make her feel more comfortable. Because she's scrunched way over in her seat to the uphill side, there's no way she'll be able to drive ahead and onto level ground.

John sees what's happening (he never misses anything, even action behind him), and has already arrived on the scene.

"Give it a little gas," he says. "And we'll help push you ahead."

"Okay," says Margy, her voice wobbly.

She advances the thumb throttle, and we ease her quad forward. Her wheels spin a bit, but in a few seconds she's safely on the wider trail ahead.

"Good work," says John, smiling at Margy through his helmet.

Coming from John, that's quite a compliment. Margy has come a long way from John's constant admonitions of "Get over it" to today's "Good work." On his scale of things, it's the ultimate compliment.

The rest of the climb goes without incident, although the deep snow temporarily halts John. He makes three attempts at one spot before he finally blasts his way through. For us, who follow in his tracks, it's a relatively easy ride in four-wheel drive.

At the end of the road, we park near the cabin and the old repeating antenna. Originally the cabin protected batteries for the old radio transmitter below Walt Hill. Thus, the name "Walt Hilton" has been give to the partly refurbished hiker's shelter. From here, it's a brief walk to the lookout.

The view is impressive. We can see all the way north to Powell Lake and beyond. To the east, Goat Main's chain of lakes is visible: Dodd, Ireland, Windsor, and Goat. Viewpoints in this region are so numerous, it would be easy to take them for granted. But we don't.

After eating our lunch at this beautiful spot, John and Eldon walk a short section of the Sunshine Coast Trail to a location where they think a path might be blazed up to the newer radio tower. They won't tackle the climb today, but they're convinced it can be hiked. (Two

days later, John returns with his brother Rick, and they make it to the top.)

We start back down on our quads, taking some time to explore the small ponds we passed on the way up. We hike back to the larger pond,

walking carefully out on the thin ice, stopping to evaluate its thickness at a few open holes. The verdict is this ice will barely hold us. But the water isn't deep, so the worst case scenario is cold, wet feet.

John and Eldon try matching their skating-on-boots skills on the ice, running as fast as possible and then sliding as far as they can go. Depending on whom you ask, they both claim victory. Constantly competitive with each other, their contest ends with a snowball fight – they both claim victory, of course.

I hike to the other end of the biggest pond, looking up at the precipice where the radio tower sits. It's a beautiful spot on a winter day, pristine beauty in the high country. The ponds exemplify the quiet remoteness found in hundreds of places like this where winter settles in with a silent beauty.

We navigate back down the old road to a turnoff where Eldon remembers another lookout he visited years ago. He leads us along the short unmarked trail to an overlook at the edge of an old logging slash. From here we can see all the way south over Lois Lake to Texada Island and across the Strait of Georgia to Vancouver Island. To the west, we look back towards Duck Lake and down to Hammil Lake near the airport.

Time is running out on this short November day. We shouldn't pause for long. Darkness will overtake us fast this time of year. To the

east, an almost-full moon is rising, looking big and white above the distant tall trees. If we start down now, we'll make it back to our trucks before sunset. Then again, a nearly full moon would provide enough light to ride even longer.

But as much as we love riding, we are people on a schedule. So we return to our quads, and start back down Granite Lake 6.

Chapter 10

Cabin Huntin'

One of John's goals when planning a quad ride involves old cabins. Over the years, he's discovered many abandoned sites in the wilderness, ideal places to explore for artifacts inside the structures and near the dwellings. Similarly, he seeks out old logging camps, farms, steam donkeys, and logging railroads that blend so well into the forest they are easily passed by without notice. But they don't escape John's constant vigilance and eagle eyes.

When he hears someone discussing an old historic site, he listens closely and asks a barrage of questions. Usually there are no real answers to his inquiries, but almost always he extracts enough information to get started in the right direction. With only a general description of the location, he's able to hone in on the site.

It's a unique process of elimination. John knows the region's roads and trails so well he can often pinpoint a cabin hidden in the woods with only a few hints to guide him. He remembers in minute detail the many places he has visited on his quad (or his motorcycle in previous decades), so he knows where the historic site "isn't." That limits the possibilities when you're seeking an elusive spot in the bush. An amazing set of eyes also helps.

"The old farm is supposed to border the river," he once told me when looking for an old site. "But I explored all the way along the south side of the river years ago, so it must be on the north side. And I've ridden all the way down to the lake from here, so it must be up the river on this side. We'll find it."

And we did locate the farm. John knew all the places where it wasn't. So it was a simple process (for him) to find out where it was.

* * * * *

Our hunt for the old cabin near Olsen's Lake begins in a local lumber store, where John meets Ernie in the power tools aisle. They discuss a rumoured cabin, comparing notes. The RCMP burned the few remaining buildings at Olsen's Lake in the 1960s, thirty years after the village was abandoned. The structures became a haven for American draft dodgers and hippies, so the historic site was almost completely demolished. A single remaining cabin, a short distance from the village, was supposedly missed in the burning spree.

The cabin's exact location is unknown to both Ernie and John, but their combined knowledge gives them additional hints. They agree to try to find it on Saturday. John will travel with Margy and me, while Ernie's friends will go with him. We'll explore separately, but both groups of riders will use the smidgens of information John and Ernie share at the store to reach the desired location.

* * * * *

Margy and I are supposed to meet John at his house at 9:15 on a mid-March morning, and we are solidly on schedule as we hook up to the quad trailer at the airport. By the time, we get to John's house, we should be right on time.

I ask Margy to pull ahead in her truck so I can check out the trailer's tail-lights. Suddenly, Bro comes charging straight me in his here-I-am excited welcome run.

"Hey, Bro! What are you doing here?"

I know John must have just come through the airport gate and will appear in just a few moments. Sure enough, there's John, with a big smile on his face.

"We're right on time," I say. "Must be you're anxious to get going."

"Oh, I was all loaded up, so I figured I'd meet you here," he says.

After checking the lights, I hop aboard Margy's quad, positioned on the front of the trailer. Then I yell to her like a rodeo cowboy: "Let's go!"

John walks fast-paced beside the trailer as Margy drives her truck, our trailer, and a cowboy on a quad towards the Flying Club exit. John and Bro beat us there, opening the gate for us so we can drive right through. We stop outside the fence, near John's truck.

"Meet you at the gas station," I say, as I hop off the quad and get into the truck with Margy.

"See you there," says John. "Don't forget, we've got to pay before we pump."

Paying first at gas stations is a recent addition to the deteriorating quality of life in Powell River. Of course, we're used to this in the States, but John considers it an unnecessary step when gassing up. Since many of the town's gas stations don't have credit card readers at the pumps, it's a bit cumbersome, especially when you have two trucks and three quads.

At the gas station, we pull into our customary positions, John on one side of the marine gas pump, with his quad in the back of his truck. We pull in on the other side with our trailer.

"My treat today," Margy says to John. "Fill up your truck and quad, and I'll pay."

"I wonder if you'll need five trips into the store for five vehicles," I joke.

While Margy walks over to the mini-store, John tries to turn the pump on. Nothing happens.

"This is the worst thing they've done in a long time," he laments. "Don't even trust us."

He flicks the pump switch on and off repeatedly, until it finally reacts when Margy makes her deposit. I turn on the marine gas pump and extend the long hose to the trailer to fuel up our two quads while John gases up his truck. When I'm finished, I hand the hose to John and flip off the pump switch.

"You shouldn't have done that," says John. "Now the pump is dead again."

John waves at the woman working behind the counter in the store, and she yells back over a blaring overhead speaker: "Sorry, you'll have to come back to the office so I can swipe your card again!"

"Figures," says John.

Margy, who has just returned to the gas island, heads back to the store.

With the embarrassing overhead speaker now silent only a few seconds, an ambulance roars down Joyce Avenue and turns down

Alberni, siren blaring. Bro immediately goes into the ungodly howl that's always set off by sirens. He howls in concert with the rushing ambulance.

The gas station's loudspeaker was loud and aggravating. The ambulance siren is ear-piercing and annoying. Bro's loud howl is, of course, booming and cute.

It doesn't take Margy five trips into the store to pay for the fuel, but it does take three.

* * * * *

John and I ride in his truck, with Bro plopped down between us. Margy follows in her truck, pulling our two quads.

We pull off Highway 101 onto Southview Road. In just a few hundred metres, a group of trucks sit at the side of the road, unloading quads.

"There's Ernie," says John.

We slow down and wave, but we don't stop. I know about John's conversation with Ernie in the power tools aisle, and there's a hint here. Although we are all looking for the same cabin, John intends to find it first, and Ernie and his friends are already off-loading their quads. We'd better keep moving.

Maybe that explains why John met us at the airport. A few minutes can make a big difference in a friendly race. No one is as competitive as John, and he usually wins.

Farther up the road, we pull over at a wide turnout, and wait for Margy. We get out of John's truck to guide her into the parking spot.

As the trailer rolls to a stop, John spies something behind its left wheel. With his amazing vision, he never misses a thing.

"The mud flap is falling off," he says. "And the bolt on the flap holds the license plate on."

While John is working on tightening the bolt, Ernie arrives, leading four other quads. They stop briefly, and we talk for a few minutes. Then they are quickly gone. I wonder if Ernie also considers this a race.

"I'm gonna go farther up the road to off-load," says John. "Bro is getting older, and this'll be a long quad ride. I'll wait for you there."

"Okay, we'll catch up," I reply.

Margy and I are ready to ride fairly promptly. Our quads should be able to travel faster than John's truck on a potholed dirt road like this one, so we shouldn't keep him waiting too long.

As we pull in behind John's truck, he's off-loaded and ready to go. Bro is running around in circles in his customary madman greeting. As I get off my quad, John notices something under the rear of my bike, and bends down to inspect it.

"Take a look at this," he says. "Not good."

He motions towards a mud-covered rubber boot on the inboard side of my right rear wheel. It looks normal to me.

"The clamp is broken on the boot," says John. "It's your CV joint, so you don't want any dirt to get in there."

"What's a CV joint?" I ask.

"The constant velocity connection. We'll need to take your wheel off."

When I look close at the boot, I notice the clamp is pulled out away from the wheel. And the small metal clasp is broken and hanging loose.

"How did you ever find that?" I ask. "I have to be right up close to even see the broken clamp."

"Oh, I'm always looking for things like that. Got to keep an eye out for stuff like this."

True, but John's eagle vision never ceases to amaze me. I'm also impressed with how quickly he jacks up my bike, pulls off the wheel, and installs a plastic tie wrap as a temporary fix. Maybe the fact that Ernie is already in front of us speeds the repair even more.

"That'll do for now," says John. "Keep an eye on it today, but it should be okay until we get home."

This is a maintenance pit stop that consumes only a few minutes. Soon we are on the trail into Theodosia, pushing along steadily, but I fall behind at several places as I take notes for this chapter. John is used to this, but I can tell he's anxious to get going again when I catch up each time.

John and Margy wait for me at the uphill path leading towards the steep park-like trail that winds upward to the ridge between Lancelot Inlet and Theodosia Valley. John goes first, followed by Margy, and then me.

This section of the trail requires four-wheel-drive, and the ruts are full of water. It splashes over my feet, coming through the open-lattice running boards until my socks feel damp, and the ride has barely begun. I've worn a pair of boots today that aren't waterproof, and I knew it when I put them on. I foolishly expected a dry ride (you should always expect wet on a quad), so now I'm paying the price. My boots look spiffy with their zipper fasteners, but they weren't a wise decision for today's ride. I carry a spare pair of socks, so I can change later. In the meantime, it's a good day to keep my feet up above the running boards when I go through water, though I should have thought of it earlier.

At the top of the ridge, we ride along a wide trail leading to the rough path that drops down to the logging dock. We're now in Theodosia Valley, headed for Olsen's Lake and a cabin few have ever seen.

* * * * *

I'm expecting Theodosia Valley to be busy today. There's lots of snow in the high country, limiting the places you can ride. Additionally,

logging activity is intense this winter, and several main trails are closed to our use. Theo is one of the few places where riding is easy, and already we've seen Ernie and his friends, so I expect quite a bit of traffic here today. (As it turns out, other than Ernie's group, we don't see another person all day long. It's amazing how pleasantly solitary this vast network of logging roads and trails can be, nearly every day of the year.)

We travel on Theodosia Main, northeastward towards Olsen's Lake, where we hope to find the old cabin. From there we plan to drop down to Powell Lake at Olsen's Landing, a picturesque spot I've visited by boat many times, but only once by quad. Margy has never taken the overland route to Olsen's Landing, so this will be quite a treat for her.

We make a stop so John can wrap Bro's head in his warm "granny cap," a soft cloth covering to keep him comfortable on a day that started out mostly sunny but has now turned cold, cloudy, and blustery. John's latest design in dog hats, perfected over the past year, has finally resulted in a version reluctantly accepted by Bro.

As we approach Olsen's Lake, John checks ardently along the side of the road where he hopes to catch a glimpse of the old cabin. John slows, scouting intensely, then suddenly sees something.

He speeds off in front of us, and turns his quad down the next logging spur. He rides standing up, looking nearly straight ahead, stopping when he reaches the end of the short path. When I pull up next to him, he's all smiles.

"Do you see it?" he asks, pointing towards a grove of trees in the distance.

I stare intently, and now I see it – a mossy, green roof and the outline of a partially collapsed cabin, almost hidden in the trees.

"Let's go!" he says. "I hear quads. Ernie could be here any minute."

I hear nothing, but John's hearing is as acute as his eyesight. He starts off through the logging slash, and Margy follows behind him. I decide to bring my author's notebook up to date first, so I sit on my quad for a few minutes longer. John is making fast progress through the difficult terrain, never easy in a logging slash full of fallen trees, cut-up logs, mud puddles, thick bushes, and briars. Margy is way behind, slowly climbing over logs and around the bushes and puddles.

"Hurry up!" I hear John yell to Margy. "They're coming!"

Sure enough, as I sit on my bike, I hear the approaching quads. Then I see Ernie leading his group down the spur to our parking spot.

I wonder how we managed to get ahead of them on Theodosia Main – they must have turned off briefly on a spur while we passed.

Ernie and his friends are off their bikes quickly, hiking towards the grove of trees surrounding the old cabin. I join them, slogging through the slash.

I catch up with Margy, but John is already inside the cabin. When he comes out, he holds a galvanized oil can with a classic old-fashioned shape.

"Look at this!" he yells back to Margy and me. "You'll like this place."

We already do like this place. It's an amazing slice of regional history, even from a distance. The roof is mostly collapsed, but it seems safe enough to go inside. We explore the cabin for about an hour, discussing what our joint knowledge can reveal about this residence. Ernie thinks this is the old Harper cabin, where Powell River's first millionaire found solitude in the 1920s.

"Harper lived in town part of the time," says Ernie. "He'd take his boat up Powell Lake to Olsen's Landing. From there, he drove an old Model T up here."

It's a wonderful glimpse into the past, and John has led us right to it. And he won the race.

* * * * *

Back at our quads, we eat lunch. Terry, one of Ernie's friends, tells Margy and me about his childhood at the Shinglemill, where he lived before the big mill fire. Where the pub and marina now sit, there was a booming village to support the production of finished shingles.

While we talk with Terry, it begins to hail – not large hailstones, but big enough to cause us to don our quad helmets. The brief storm is over in a few minutes, but it reminds us today's weather won't achieve the sunny forecast, at least not here in Theodosia Valley.

After Ernie and his friends depart, John leads us back onto the main and down towards Olsen's Landing. I visualize an old Model T climbing up this dirt road nearly a hundred years ago.

We pass piles of shake-blocks lying alongside the road. Some are loosely roped together, while others are arranged on pallets. These shakes were dragged here by shake blockers or dropped by helicopter from the surrounding logging sites. They'll be picked up by truck and hauled to Olsen's Landing for barge transport down Powell Lake to

Block Bay. Someday soon they'll be wooden shingles for roofs around the world.

Olsen's Main is an easy and majestic ride, winding down along Olsen's Creek to the logging dock at the landing where work machines of all types and sizes are parked. The final descent is particularly spectacular, with views of Powell Lake breaking through the surrounding forest. Near the dock, a barge-size load of palletized shakes sits next to a big blue crane mounted on a truck.

Rather than stop at the dock, John leads us around the point to the right, where a small campsite sits on a patch of mossy ground. John stops only long enough to help Bro out of his aft quad box. Then he roars off on his bike to play on the delta. Bro runs beside him – two kids playing on the beach.

Margy and I park our quads on the mossy area and share a can of pop.

"It's an amazing lake," says Margy.

From any angle, any time of the year, Powell Lake is our personal paradise. As the seasons progress, we never tire of the lake's changing features. I snap a photo in an attempt to duplicate the scene that

appeared on the cover of my first book about quad riding, *Up the Main*. Clouds and low visibility limit today's view of the lake. In these weather conditions, it's still enchantingly beautiful.

The previous book cover photo was taken on a clear summer afternoon, not a blustery March day like this. The summer scene was a majestic mix of water, mountains, and a brilliant blue sky. That was four years ago. This spot hasn't changed. Yet, the seasons and daily weather make places like this seem different every day.

When John returns from the beach, he and Margy explore around the campsite. They find tracks of Roosevelt Elk released here only a few months ago. It's part of a relocation project, an ongoing attempt to introduce elk to locations where they can thrive. Thanks to the dedicated people involved in this program, including the Powell River ATV Club, elk numbers are increasing in our region.

John finds a driftwood guitar carefully constructed by a logger or camper who obviously had lots of time on his hands. The strings are made of thin rope, and the ring of an old metal can forms a fake opening to the non-existent acoustical chamber. Elvis John throws the rope guitar strap over his shoulder and croons us a tune.

The days are short in March, so we need to start back. John still has several stops planned along the way, so we can't delay any longer.

First comes Dalgleish Main. This is a logging road I explored with John on my first quad ride in the area. It's a mountain goat paradise

and a beautiful climb. But ever since I mentioned my desire to revisit this road earlier today, John has been hesitant. I'm not sure why, but maybe it's because of the snow expected in the high country. Yet, John loves to play in the snow with his quad.

"Do the goats stay up in the snow this time of year?" I ask.

"No, they come down lower," he replies. "Impossible to see in the trees."

So maybe that's it. Although he agrees to start up the logging road, he lacks his normal enthusiasm.

The initial climb is easy, like any other active logging road. But this isn't an active road, and the path soon deteriorates to a rocky surface, jagged, heavily rutted, and rough. When we stop at an overlook that lets us peer down on Powell Lake and Olsen's Landing, I comment on the road condition.

"The road's a mess," I say. "Like a dry creek bed that has run wild."

"It's a roaring creek after a rain," says John. "Since they deactivated this road, it's really deteriorated. Usually the logging company cuts cross-ditches to carry off the water. It prevents big gouges and washouts. But not here."

That's not it either, since John likes the challenges of deep cross-ditches. But his lack of enthusiasm for this challenging trail is obvious in his voice.

We spend a few minutes sitting on the edge of the drop-off, looking down on a logging slash and the lake below.

When we get going again, we're almost immediately stopped by a washout that crosses the trail. The natural cross-ditch drops off precipitously on the downhill side, so we stop to repair the damage.

There are lots of rocks near the ditch that we can move into the low side of the trench. We dig around and build up the rut until John feels it's safe. Our three-person (plus a dog) road crew makes a quick but efficient repair, and we're on our way again, It takes four-wheel-drive to get across the repaired area, but it's a comfortable and safe crossing.

We enter an area of alders where thick branches stick out from the trees growing along the side of the trail. The farther we go, the worse it gets. Thank goodness for helmets and goggles to protect our heads and eyes in this extensive thicket. John stops a few times, using his position in the lead to whack at the branches, breaking some off.

So this is it! – I should've known. John hates alders, and our ride has turned into a battle with these pesky trees that quickly take over inactive logging roads.

Patches of snow appear along the trail, but they are still only a minor obstacle when we reach a spot where the alders consume the whole trail. John stops and begins to turn around. Margy and I also maneuver our quads to reverse course on the narrow trail. We're quickly out of the alders and back down to clear road. John can handle rough trails and snow. But he can't handle the dreaded alders, unless it's a trail-building project with the promise of a tangible goal. And he knew this trail would be obstructed, even though he hasn't been here in recent months. The view down to Powell Lake is spectacular, but the tradeoff of battling alders makes it barely worth it.

We wind back down to Olsen's Lake, where we park on the wide gravel beach at the north end. We enjoy a snack of cookies and pop, looking out over this beautiful small lake.

After our brief stop, John leads us to the spot where the Theodosia River enters the lake. For a brief stretch, we battle mud holes. John makes it through one of the wettest spots easily. When Margy starts to follow, I yell to her.

"Keep your feet up off your running boards!"

She nods *Yes*, and then starts through. She plows through the water, her quad doing an admirable job in almost any terrain, including wet spots like this. John supervises her crossing from the other side, always vigilant at places where a less experienced rider might get into trouble.

After we make it through this section, we ride a few hundred metres to the place where water was diverted by the paper mill to feed its ravenous appetite for electrical power. An extensive cement diversion channel was constructed to reroute the water coming down the upper Theodosia River. Rather than continue down its natural route to Theodosia Inlet, the water was diverted into Olsen's Lake, down Olsen's Creek, into Powell Lake, and to the mill's power-producing dam at the south end. The diversion channel is a foreboding structure reminding me that the paper mill controls a lot of things around here. They even try to control nature.

"They built this just to get more electrical power?" I ask.

"Until everybody got upset enough to demand another diversion channel be built to send most of the flow back down to Theodosia Inlet. Lots of wasted time and money, if you ask me."

The second diversion channel sits to the side of the main cement structure, looking like an afterthought (which it was). Now the salmon traveling up the Theodosia River are again protected, at least relatively so.

"All for the damn dam," I say. "Just stealing more water."

Every chance I get, I pick on the mill regarding their dam at the south end of Powell Lake. My float cabin drops precariously low against the cliff of Hole in the Wall when all of the dam's gates are wide open. Sometimes it seems the mill sucks off more water than is appropriate to make electricity.

"It's called greed," says John.

A lot of us pick on the paper mill. But what would we do without it? Like most big guys, the mill is an easy target.

"Let's get going," says John. "We've got a few more stops on the way back, and it'll be getting dark soon."

Traveling with John is like going on a safari planned out in every detail, but with the ability to deviate to new destinations at a moment's notice. Margy and I follow with enthusiasm, and are never disappointed by the adventures we find.

"I'll catch up," I say, again pulling out my author's notebook.

John and Margy start off down the road, and I turn to my writing pad. What I don't know is, while I'm writing, they pass through an intersection less than 100 metres straight in front of me. Normally, John stops at every junction when I'm not in sight behind him, assuring I don't miss the intended route. But in this case, while they pass through the intersection, I'm looking down at my notes. Not surprisingly, John assumes I see which route to take, since it's easily visible from my quad. But I'm not watching.

When I catch up on my paperwork, I put my notebook away and start down the main. But almost immediately, I come to the intersection. Which way did they go?

Straight ahead seems like the obvious choice, since it heads nearly directly west. But to the right is a major bridge over the Theodosia River. There are lots of quad tracks leading to the right and over the bridge, and no tracks are visible straight ahead. On the other hand, the road straight ahead is hard-packed, and tracks would be hard to see. I get off my bike to inspect the road straight ahead for any evidence of tread marks. I see none.

Thus, my dilemma. The road straight ahead seems most logical. But tread marks go to the right. And these tracks are definitely fresh, although they could be from Ernie's group. I make a good decision – I decide to sit at this intersection and wait for John to return for me. Obviously, he'll begin to worry about me soon, and then he'll return to this spot.

So I wait. And I wait. John doesn't return for me. How could this be?

After waiting twenty minutes, the answer comes to me – John knows I might go straight here or I might turn to the right. And either road will take me to where he and Margy now sit, waiting for me. So why should he come back, if there is no bad decision at this intersection. At least that's my analysis, enhanced by my desire to do something, even if it's wrong.

The tire tracks over the bridge to the right win out. I start across the river and head north. In just a short drive, there's a Y-intersection where it seems logical to continue nearly straight ahead. Then I'm into beautiful heavily-forested terrain where loggers have recently worked. High stacks of discarded wood are piled into inverted V-shaped piles on both sides of the road. I continue, and the road leads upward and then towards the west. As far as I can tell, I've somehow missed Theodosia Main and am now headed into a dense area of the forest. But it's also beautiful, so I continue.

I've learned that dead-end logging spurs can look like main roads, particularly when they're new and well maintained. To get off a main is easier than most people would think.

I come to a dead end – my error is finally obvious. So I turn around. But first I glance at my gas gauge (which is getting low) and then at the bright area of clouds hiding the sun (which is getting lower). For a moment, I feel my heart race. I'm pretty rugged when it comes to struggling with the forest, but tonight will be cold and probably wet, and I have no camping gear.

I speed back down the logging spur, carefully retracing my path to the intersection by the river. I stop at the original intersection for a few minutes, parking at the same spot where I waited for John. Maybe he'll still appear. Or maybe he has already come here while I was gone, and left.

The hard-packed road with no visible quad tracks now seems the obvious choice. I'm sure it will take me back towards the west, eventually merging with Theodosia Main. But the sun is dropping lower, and time is my enemy.

I take off down the road, riding as fast as seems safe. I imagine John and Margy sitting beside this road, waiting for me. They'll be a pleasant sight. It's also a sight to be feared, for John doesn't take lightly to my errors in the forest. Though it seemed logical to wait at the intersection, something went wrong, and I'm probably to blame. Even if I'm not, I expect John to chew me out for something. Getting lost is inexcusable to him, no matter what the reason. And wasting his time is an equally punishable offense. So I think of excuses as I drive: "I waited for you a long time; the road to the right had fresh tracks; then I came back and tried the other road."

My speedometer shows 50 klicks, a safe speed on this well-groomed dirt road. I hope I'll find John and Margy before I get all the way back to our trucks. If I don't, everybody will be upset – specifically, both John and me.

There! – off to the right at an intersection angling in from the right! John and Margy sit on their quads, waiting for me. I'm saved!

I slow and pull off the road. John is grinning. But he motions to me, a gesture clearly showing an imaginary shotgun aimed at me. He pumps his arm, loading the imaginary pump-action gun chamber, and shoots. It's a good sign. He's mad, but he's also pleased to see me, in his own distorted way.

"Where the hell have you been?" he asks, as soon as I turn off my engine.

I hold my hands over my helmet, as if I don't want to hear him: "Now before you get all upset," I say, "don't forget there might be two sides to this story."

"So what's your side?" he says.

Margy is now standing beside her quad, laughing. Another good sign.

"I waited for a full twenty minutes at the first intersection after the diversion channel. I didn't see which way you went. When you didn't return for me, I finally tried the road that goes over the bridge."

"That's the wrong one," he says.

"So now I know. And where were you?" I accuse.

Maybe I can go on the offensive. John pauses before he replies, indicating he may not be innocent either. I've got him! And I know it.

"We were trying to find the old Japanese logging camp," says Margy. "When we got back to our bikes, we thought you'd be waiting for us."

"So did you find the camp?" I ask.

My diversionary tactics are in action. I seldom win in even the smallest battle with John, except maybe this time.

"Didn't find it," says John. "But I know it's around here someplace."

"So did you go back to Olsen's Lake looking for me?" I ask.

"Well, if you waited twenty minutes, it must've been twenty-five minutes before I got back to the intersection. I started back as soon as we noticed you were missing."

John's voice is almost apologetic. Not quite, but almost.

"There's no reason for anybody to get upset," I say. "We did what we thought was best, and what more can we ask? It's been a great day of cabin hunting, and I got to explore a bit on my own."

It's a compromise, which in my book is a victory. And so ends my hour of spatial disorientation near Olsen's Lake. I wasn't really lost, of course, but for a few minutes I was a bit unsure of my position. And I'm glad to be back with John, Margy, and Bro.

Chapter 11

Mount Mahony

When winter moves in, Mount Mahony is a quick route to heavy snow. Located just north of town, the mountain is easily accessed by conventional vehicles, at least until you start up the deactivated portion of the road to the top.

With a forecast for clearing skies, we drive in light rain to our off-load spot at an intersection near Inland Lake. For Margy and me, a little rain seems acceptable. But John joins us today only because he's convinced the rain will stop soon or we'll quickly top the clouds into clear skies above.

Margy and I follow John's pickup around the turn towards Haywire Bay, where snow starts to appear along the side of the road. The gentle incline is enough to promote a remarkably fast buildup of snow, an indicator of the heavy snow depth we expect during the climb.

As we drive our quads off the trailer, John dresses Bro in his blue raincoat and cloth wrap-around hat. The dog hesitantly accepts the attention, but he doesn't look happy in his latest version of a dog hat. It's a love-hate relationship with hats for Bro – he loves the warmth, but hates anything covering his ears. Maybe looking like a seal isn't his favourite thing either.

This near-freezing November day calls for a full-face mask under my helmet and several layers of clothes beneath my rain gear. We expect the first part of the ride to be the coldest. It will be warmer in the sun above the clouds. Unless, of course, we never get high enough.

We drive our quads north along the main road for several kilometres, and then turn off onto a forest service road marked: *Caution – Road*

Deactivated. Wide tracks in the snow show the path of several vehicles with wheelbases wider than quads. They've passed so recently their tread marks are still crisp.

When the path begins to narrow and the cross-ditches begin to deepen, we come across several sets of footprints in the snow. One set is so small I first think they belong to a dog. Then I notice these are tiny human footprints. It's not particularly surprising to see a child's prints in the snow, especially since larger adult footprints are alongside. But what is surprising is the marks continue for several kilometres.

We pass a parked Jeep surrounded by recent footprints. Farther up the trail, the marks in the snow continue, pointed both up and down the trail. Mixed with the adult prints are the child's, pointing clearly one-way – downhill.

As we round a corner, the answer is right in front of us. A dark blue pickup is stuck, blocking the road. John gets off his quad and walks to the truck.

"Got stuck here last night," says the man in the truck. "Walked back down with my young son, and came back this morning to try again."

That explains the child's tracks. Probably the Jeep was the man's source of transportation this morning. Still, it must have been a long walk out of here last night, for both man and boy.

"There's a place where you can turn around just a little ways farther up this hill," says John. "If we can get you up there."

Turning the vehicle around to face downhill at this narrow spot would be impossible. With a little shoveling and a lot of pushing, we manage to get the truck moving up the hill. Once he gets going again, the man uses full throttle to spin his way out of sight.

John and Margy restart their quads, and I wave them on while I pull my author's notebook out of my pocket to make a few scratches I hope I can read later. It's easy to write with my gloves on, but it's never very legible. I'm used to writing chapters that begin as hen scratches.

When I finally start up the hill, I immediately see the blue pickup bounding down the hill towards me. I pull as far to the side of the trail as I can to give the truck room to get by. The pickup squeezes past as I wave the driver on. He slips and slides his way down the hill, but should make it back down to where the Jeep is parked without further problems. But what is he going to do then with two vehicles? Nothing is simple when you get stuck on the side of a mountain in winter.

Our ride in the snow for the next few kilometres is a joy. The conditions are well within the limits of our quads, and tread-marks are no longer in front of us, providing an increased sense of remoteness. We ride along a wide pristine trail in the deepening snow.

We break through the top of the clouds, and it's warmer now. But a forecast calling for clearing skies below seems substantially in error. We're in the sunshine, but only because we've passed through a lingering layer of stratus clouds that covers everything as far as the eye can see.

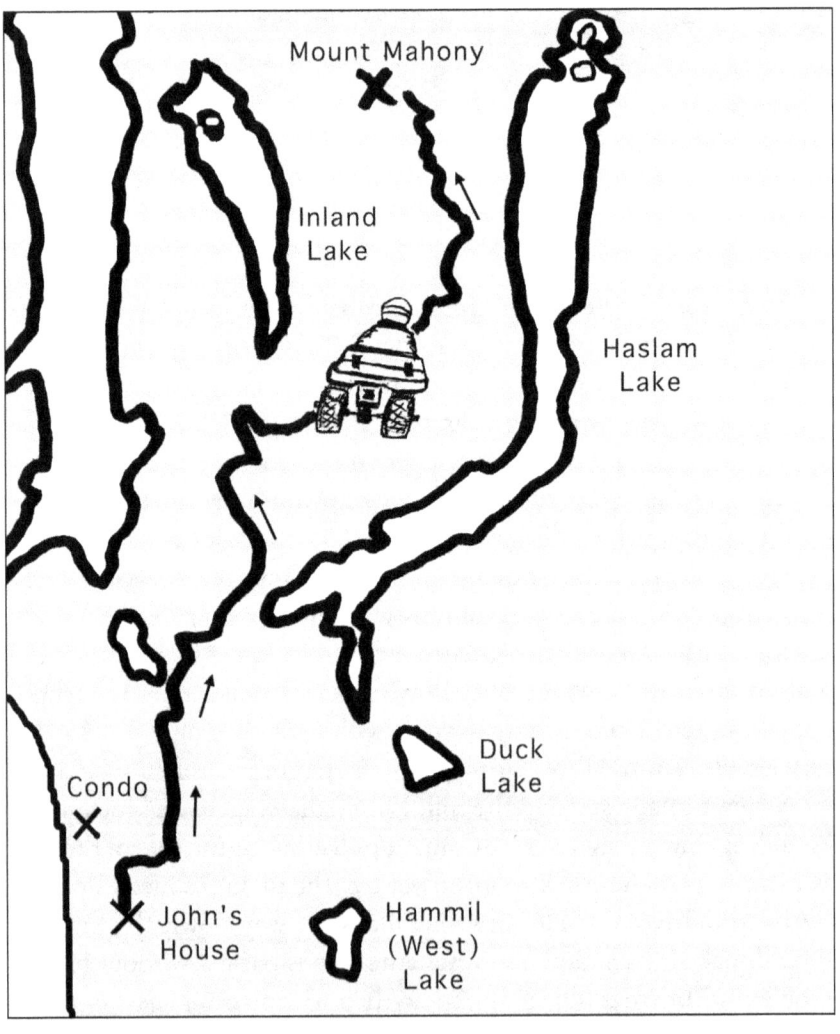

John angles over to the side of the trail, waiting for Margy and me to catch up. We pull up next to him in snow a foot deep.

"You'll need to use your lockers here," he says. "And keep you throttle wide open or you'll never make it to the top."

I'm skeptical of differential lockers. I've only engaged the switch a few times, and the handling quality of a quad is (in my opinion) adversely affected. To me, basic four-wheel drive seems as efficient as lockers in rough terrain. So I listen to what John says, and then ignore it, leaving my lockers off. I'm so smart – I'll have better steering and still make it through.

John removes Brody from his aft box, indicating the trail is going to be particularly tough. As has been repeatedly proven, when Bro is asked to walk, it means look-out-ahead.

John goes first, blasting his way out of sight. Bro goes galloping up the hill after him.

Margy follows, slowly at first. Then I watch her punch the throttle and climb solidly, although more slowly than John, upward and around the corner at the top of the hill.

Now it's my turn. I move forward only a few metres and am immediately stuck. Following in the tracks of another quad is always easier, but my four-wheel drive has let me down. I rock the bike, shifting repeatedly from forward to reverse, and finally break free of the ruts. I reluctantly shift into differential lockers and begin to make traction. As usual, John's right. As usual, I don't listen, and I pay for it.

When I catch up with Margy and John, they are laughing together at the top of the hill.

"Didn't use your lockers, did you?" says John.

"So now I know," I reply with a grimace.

"Want to go first on the next steep section?" asks John. "It's a lot harder to lead in the snow, but you should be able to make it."

I take it as a compliment. John always leads on the tough slopes, and his offer is generous. I've never pushed into snow near the limit of my quad on my own, so this should be an interesting test of my abilities. I'll make sure my lockers are engaged this time.

At the base of the next hill, John pulls over and waves me around him. This time I spare nothing with the throttle. With the added traction of the lockers, my engine revs to maximum power, and I plow through the fresh snow with a roar. In the lead, it's more exciting than

I expected. But it's not as comfortable as I thought it would be – with no tire treads to follow, especially going at full blast on the side of a mountain!

My forward momentum is steady enough that I never doubt I'll make it to the top of this hill. But without tracks to follow, I'm not exactly sure where the trail really is. Although I expect it to be obvious (as it is when following someone else), there are no markers except the flow of the land. What if I momentarily get off the trail and there's a big rock hidden beneath the snow? What if I'm on the trail but a deep cross-ditch is hidden under the thick mantle of white, waiting to toss me over the handlebars? When blasting forward at full throttle, these are thoughts best not pondered.

When the slope levels off at the top, I finally throttle back and pull forward far enough to make room for John and Margy. In a rare reversal of our normal riding sequence, Margy is next, cresting the hill like an expert. John is last to arrive, all smiles for having given us a chance to lead. Anything we accomplish at the limits of our bikes is owed to John. We know it, and so does he.

The rest of the ride to the top is a mix of easy terrain and short stretches of rugged trail. We switch in and out of differential lockers, climb slow and then fast, and bask in the sunshine.

The last push is on a portion of trail I would easily loose if I were in the lead. But John knows the path well, pressing on without ever a doubt. We drive through a grove of tall trees and punch out onto

a snow-covered bluff, where traces of the solid granite cap protrude through the drifts.

Looking out over the edge of the snowy bluff, the view is an indistinct merger of snow cover and the white tops of clouds. It looks like you could step out onto the clouds. But that would be a mighty big leap.

We relax on the bluff for nearly an hour, a prolonged lunch stop with majestic views over the cloud-covered land. We look south, out over the chuck and down on a small lake nestled in a hidden valley in the forest.

We've been in the sunshine for several hours now. This short November day is drawing to a close, and we'll need to start down through the clouds without any further delay. Below us, we know it's getting dark. And down there, it's still damp, probably raining. But up here, the sky seems endlessly blue.

We climb back onto our quads and start on our way again, with the shadow of the mountain following us down.

◊ ◊ ◊ ◊ ◊ ◊ ◊

Chapter 12

Last Chance

I phone John shortly after 9 am. He rode all day yesterday, including many hours of trail building with his brother, Rick, so I don't expect he'll be interested in riding again today.

"Hi, Rick," I say, when I recognize his voice on the line.

When he answers John's phone this early in the morning, it's likely John is still asleep.

"How'd you do yesterday?" I ask. "Is the trail finished?"

"Not quite," says Rick. "But we had time for a ride up Alaska Pine. Still a few patches of snow – a nice ride."

"So John's not up yet?" I ask.

"Oh, he's outside, loading his quad. I'll get him."

So John's going riding, after all. I was looking forward to a leisurely ride with him tomorrow, but not today. It's already too late to come down the lake, hook up my quad trailer, and get going. Besides, today is probably another trail-building project, which can be particularly grueling. He and Rick have been working is a remote, rough, and somewhat secret location. They like to get some personal use out of trail they've fixed up before it's used by other riders. Trails repaired by the two brothers are always a fine product, so you'd think they'd be pleased to have everyone use it right away. They enjoy the compliments on their hard work, but they also like getting some personal enjoyment from the fruits of their labour first.

"Where are you going today?" I ask when John comes to the phone.

"You know where. Just some touch-up work on the trail. Wanna come?"

"I'm still up the lake," I reply, "So I wouldn't be able to get hooked up to my trailer in time."

"Right. I'm just about to leave."

"What about tomorrow. Would another day in a row be too much for you?"

By "you," I really mean Bro, since too many days in a row on a quad can be trouble for the big Lab. His old hips get strained on a tough ride. Not only does he bounce away in his aft quad box, he often has to walk through the rough spots. Trail-building is even more demanding, with Bro running up and down the slopes to keep up with John.

"Hey, do you hear that clicking?" asks John. "Somebody's on the line."

"I hear it. Sounds like someone trying to steal your trail location."

"Seriously, do you hear it? Somebody's listening in."

There is someone else on the line, trying to dial. It could be my cell phone connection or another phone at John's house. I seriously doubt it's a trail spy.

"Don't be paranoid," I chide. "What about a nice easy ride with me tomorrow. That would be good for Bro."

"Call me tonight. Right now I gotta' get going."

"Sure, no problem. Have a good ride."

"I still hear clicking on the line," says John, with a touch of nervousness. "What is it?"

"Don't know. Probably a trail spy."

* * * * *

That night, I phone John again. It isn't easy to get through. When his phone is busy like this, I know he's working on setting up a big ride for tomorrow. Riding with groups isn't my favourite thing, especially when a more personal ride with John allows me to get his full attention as he shows me what he knows about the great outdoors. And what he knows is truly amazing.

After repeated attempts, I finally get through.

"Sounds like you've been holding court tonight," I say.

"Oh, just trying to get some guys together to work on the Last Chance Trail. Wanna' come?"

Now this is a dilemma. As indisposed as I am to riding with groups, and as much as I realize how demanding John's work parties can be, I really want the Last Chance Trail to be improved. It's a great shortcut to Powell Lake's Chippewa Bay and then to Hole in the Wall. The other route (through Theodosia Valley) is a lot longer, and now that trail has been destroyed by logging. Already, another trail has been built, and I haven't seen it yet, but I hear it's very rough and probably beyond Margy's riding capabilities. That means the land route to our cabin, at least for now, is cut off. Thus, the Last Chance Trail is particularly important. So far I've never tried it, but with a little work, maybe it'll be useable for cabin access.

"Man, I'm glad you're working on that trail," I say. "It'd be great to make it accessible to amateurs like Margy and me. But maybe that's not possible."

"Can't work miracles," replies John. "It's in bad shape after the winter. We'll never be able to get rid of some of those steep sections. For now, at least we can make it passable."

"I'd like to help. So count me in. But what about Bro?"

"I'm not sure yet. Maybe I should leave him home. He's had some rough rides the past few days."

"What time do you plan to leave?" I ask.

"Can you be at my house at ten?"

"You can count on it."

"So see you then."

* * * * *

The next morning, a partly cloudy day in early June, I awaken at 5 am, well before the alarm goes off. I dial in the financial news on the satellite radio, awaiting the scheduled 5:30 release of employment statistics. These are rocky economic times, and I'm fascinated by all of the commotion in the stock market and the entire global situation. I expect I'll never see a more tumultuous time in the economy, and I've been watching things closely for years. It affects all of us personally, but the broad economic picture is also enthralling to me.

This morning, CNBC confirms the optimism everyone has been touting lately regarding the expected job numbers. Supposedly, it'll be a turning point in this economic mess. And maybe the stock markets will finally start climbing again.

Since I'm awake, why not get up and get going? I could lay in bed and try to go back to sleep, or I could climb downstairs from the loft and listen to the economic reports on the sofa. Since this is a cool June morning, I'll need to build a fire if I go downstairs. So why not just get dressed and get going?

I gather up my riding gear, put on multiple layers of clothes, including long-johns (in June!), and pack up my laptop. Since I'll get to town early, I can check my email and get some Internet jobs accomplished, using their wireless access.

I'm ready to go now, but the jobs news release is only a few minutes away, so I plop down on the sofa to catch the report. It's not good news. The expected numbers for U.S. unemployment are a disaster, and the Dow Jones average plummets immediately on the report. Maybe I should resolve that my attention to the news isn't helping a bit.

Ten minutes after six, I'm motoring out of Hole in the Wall, and by the time I reach the North Sea, I'm in sunlight. The sun is well above the horizon early this time of year.

At the airport, I hook up the quad trailer, deciding to take both bikes with me. I'd have plenty of time to off-load Margy's quad, but that would mean unstrapping and unloading a quad that would need to be reloaded and retied when I return. This will cause some concern when John discovers I'm taking an extra quad into the bush, exposed to the rest of the world, so I double-lock the bike farthest forward on the trailer (mine), using a heavy chain and a smaller cable. Today I'll use Margy's quad, conveniently parked in the back.

After finding a nice double parking spot behind the hotel, I make myself comfortable in the lobby to check my email. It seems like an amazingly efficient morning so far, and I'm well ahead of schedule.

At 9 o'clock, I call John just to make sure he still wants me at his house at 10:00. Sometimes, when he's coordinating a group of riders, things change fast. John doesn't appreciate it when I'm lax in my attitude towards getting started. He's used to moving quickly, and off-loading and getting on the trail even faster. When I keep him waiting, I'm often reminded that I'm always the perpetual slowpoke.

"Still on schedule?" I ask.

"Sure. Are you in town already?"

"I've been here for hours, ready to go," I reply. "You're always holding me up."

That's dangerous to say. I'm always the one running behind, and John is always prodding me to "Hurry up." If I challenge him in this game, I'll surely lose.

"I need breakfast first," I say. "But I'm still ahead of you." (Another unwise boast I'll probably pay for.) "I'll swing by McDonald's, then meet you at the gas station instead of your house, although I've already gassed up my quad."

The fast-food restaurant and the gas station are next to each other. It really isn't true that I've already stopped for gas, but I'll let John think I'm far ahead of him. Actually, I plan to empty the spare gas can on the back of Margy's bike into her tank, which should fill it up.

"You're not ahead of me," says John. "If we miss each other at the gas station, I'll meet you on Southview Road. I'll probably beat you."

"Doubt it," I say.

The silence on the other end of the phone tells me my strategy is definitely backfiring.

* * * * *

Leaving the hotel, I head to Canada Post. It takes only a few moments to haul the trailer past the drive-through mailboxes, and drop off some letters. Then I park across the street at the bank (double spot again) and use the automated teller to deposit a check. I don't want John to beat me, but I need to get some things accomplished before I leave town. Knowing John, this will be a long day on the trail, and I want to make it back up the lake before dark. Never waste any sunlight in the morning when you're with John. The other end of the day can get pretty dark.

When I come out of McDonald's after my quick breakfast, I drive from one side of the Golden Arches around to the other, where the gas station sits. John's truck, with his quad in back, is parked at the marine gas aisle.

By the time I pull into the parking area next to the gas station, John is walking back to his truck from the station's mini-mart. I park the trailer awkwardly between the white lines, leaving the rear sticking out at an angle that won't please John.

"Have you pumped your gas yet?" I ask.

"No. I just paid. Bastards don't trust me."

The new requirement to pay before you pump still aggravates John. Me too – reminds me of the States.

"Just need to grab some snacks in the store," I say.

I stop at his truck briefly to pet Bro, who is hopping up and down in the front seat, nearly jumping out of the window, in his typical "Hello!" mode.

"Terry and I will park just beyond the stop sign on Southview Road," says John. "Near the old trailer."

"Okay. I'll probably use the wide turnout on the lower end of Southview. It works good for the trailer."

"We'll find each other."

John actually sounds a little gruff, maybe because of my boastful kidding this morning.

"Sure," I say, as I head for the mini-mart to buy some lunch snacks.

As I walk towards the store, I glance back at John and notice him looking over my trailer and its two quads. He doesn't say anything about my bringing Margy's quad along, but I know what he's thinking. And, undoubtedly, my amateur parking job doesn't please him either.

I spend only a few minutes buying some chips, a pop, and a small package of cookies. By the time I leave the store, John's truck is already gone.

* * * * *

I park at the wide turnout on Southview Road. As soon as I turn off the truck's motor, I hear a vehicle approaching from behind. Terry rumbles to a stop in his truck, with his quad in back.

"Two quads?" says Terry.

Like John, he has a practical view of operations in the backcountry. Everyone still thinks of me as city-folk, and they're not entirely wrong.

"Never know when you might need a spare," I kid. "Heck, when I go on a ride, I've got all of the spare parts I could possibly need – starter, tires, you name it."

Terry laughs. But I bet he knows John won't like it.

"Have you seen John yet?" asks Terry.

"Near the gas station, but he left before me. He's probably ahead of us, already at the parking spot near the stop sign."

"I doubt it," says Terry. "I think he's behind me."

"Probably not," I reply. "He's punishing me."

"Punishing you? Why?"

"Hasn't he ever punished you when you're slow? This morning I told him he was holding me up."

"Never say that," says Terry.

He knows John well.

"Well I just had to. But I never win."

Just then, John's old truck rattles up. Now Terry and John are two abreast on the narrow dirt road, engines running, while my truck and trailer cover the shoulder.

"We've been here talking for a half hour," I tease. "Just waiting for you."

"Yeah, right," replies John.

We gab for a few minutes, completely blocking the road. Then again, there isn't any traffic.

When John and Terry leave, I hurry to get my quad off the trailer. It's nearly certain they'll be parked and waiting for me at the stop sign. Me, the notorious slowpoke.

But the faster I go, the further behind I get. I'm used to Margy helping me with the off-load. We work well together as a coordinated team, completing our own self-assigned tasks. Today I do both of our duties, but forget some of them. I lock the truck's rear canopy, and then find an extra tiedown strap that needs to be put away. After putting it in the truck and locking the canopy again, I notice my lunch is missing, so I unlock the truck and retrieve it. Finally I'm ready to ride.

I zoom up Southview Road, able to travel comfortably at 50 klicks on the straight stretches, since there are few potholes. When I pull into the spot where Terry and John have parked. John is already on his quad, helmet on, Bro loaded, and ready to go.

"Where've you been?" asks John.

"Figures," I say. "Never try to beat John."

The cloud of dust from my arrival swirls past us. I think I see a smile within John's helmet. The race is over, and I lost again.

"Look at the dust," says John.

"Just like summer," I reply.

It's an indicator today will require leaving enough space between riders to keep out of dirt clouds. Although it's been a wet spring, road conditions are drying up and getting dusty.

"Finally ready?" asks John.

"Ready!" is my brusque reply.

Fortunately, Terry is delaying our departure. He's sauntering around the parking area, adjusting his helmet and gloves, maybe trying to slow John down. I think he's trying to help me look like the winner, but it's futile.

* * * * *

Once we're underway, Terry leads, followed by John (and Bro, of course), and I bring up the rear. We head up the forest service road that leads east from the stop sign, steeply climbing towards the Bunster Range. My dust-length behind John is about 100 metres, close enough to occasionally catch sight of his Grizzly. Along the way, newly posted yellow signs with stark black lettering mark each kilometre. These are classy looking signs, much brighter and more professional than others you see on logging roads. Each sign proclaims in large letters: "Thedosia Forest Service Road, Branch 1," with Theodosia misspelled on every sign. On Branch 2 that runs north from the same stop sign, the new signs are similarly misspelled. I wonder if the guy who mass-produced them even knows what he did?

We pass the wide turnoff that marks the majestic point looking down on Okeover Inlet. John slows in front of me, and takes a rolling look. I do the same, coming almost to a stop to enjoy the view.

The dust finally ends when we cross Appleton Creek and pull off the mainline onto the path leading up towards the start of the Last Chance Trail. We climb into the upper Bunsters, following an easy trail to the old slash where huge trunks span a vast open area.

Mike is waiting for us in a wide turnoff, framed by slabs of rock and a seemingly endless field of old cut cedar trunks. I've never ridden with Mike before, but I quickly learn he's very accomplished on a quad. While we're talking, his dad pulls up to join us.

Jim is even more experienced in the woods than his son. He's a retired logger, and remembers today's route from his days building logging roads that have now been reclaimed by nature. Jim and Mike are fun to watch. Father and son banter comfortably – two guys of separate eras who know the backcountry in different ways.

Our quads, now five in number, continue up the path through the logging slash, where we find a sign to our right that reads "Last Chance." Terry is one of the ATV Club's trail sign builders, and this is his work. Based on the fine quality of the sign, you'd think you're entering a well-established trail. It's definitely a far cry from that.

I remember several years earlier when Margy and I followed John, Dave, and Rick up into this slash. At the time, the three brothers were trying to trailblaze, looking for a path that would connect down to Chippewa Bay. They had attempted several routes previously, without getting beyond an area of dense marsh and scattered ponds (*Up the Main*, Chapter 10.)

"We're gonna' give it one more go," Dave declared that day. "And if it doesn't work this time, we'll have to give up. It's really our last chance."

"Last Chance," repeated John. "That's what we'll call it, when we finally get through."

"You mean: if we get through," corrected Rick

"When," challenged John.

These days, local ATV riders hold the Last Chance Trail in considerable awe. It's a route through an exceptionally rugged area that can only be improved so much.

"One of the roughest trails I've ever ridden," notes Mario, a guy who has seen a whole bunch of very rough trails.

But I often ask myself: "How rough can it be?" Others have ridden through it, and I've become a relatively accomplished rider in recent years. If we can groom this trail enough to make it passable for Margy, whose riding abilities are good but a bit fragile at times, we'll have a quick route to Hole in the Wall. How rough can it be? – I find out almost immediately after entering the trail.

Right away, we're slogging through mud and deep ruts, accompanied by steep curvy sections that seem beyond hope. It's obviously four-wheel-drive territory, so I stop briefly and hit the switch, watching the 4-wheel icon illuminate on my instrument panel. Rocks and roots protrude everywhere, providing challenges to our abilities and hazards to our bikes. We pass through this first difficult area without stopping to fix anything, so we can get to the "really bad" spots where we'll need to work. In other words, it gets a lot worse.

As usual, when the going gets tough, Bro has to walk so John can properly maneuver his bike. It's best for John and best for the dog. The black Lab scampers before us on the trail, showing an initial blast of energy. By tonight, his legs will be tired, just like my arms and shoulders from fighting the handle bars on rough sections. Terry's bike has the luxury of power steering, while John and I fight the turns the old fashioned way. I'm not sure about Mike and Jim, but their newer-looking quads probably have power steering, too. Plus, everybody here today, except for me, is a backwoods expert.

John comes to a stop on a rare level section and motions for me to pull up close behind him.

"Need to get close," he says. "We need to fit all of our bikes in this short stretch so we can work on the trail ahead."

The trail ahead has a significant drop – fairly straight but with protruding roots and rocks leading to several drop-offs that need to be groomed. It's not the worst of what we'll find on this trail today, but it needs some work. After swinging a pick-axe for a while, I take a break to snap a few photos of the rest of our crew working under Bro's supervision. Like all the photos I take today, I'm amazed when I review them at home. The trail doesn't look that bad. Maybe it's because I couldn't stop and shoot pictures in the worst spots. Or maybe it's just because you had to be there to grasp the severe roughness.

Farther down the trail, we approach one of the ugliest-looking hills, rutted on all sides and obviously requiring a lot of power to climb. John stops in front of me and yells back: "Lockers!"

I nod my head, not being surprised this slope will require the use of differential wheel lock. It's not a switch I use often, since it greatly degrades steering control. Turning a quad with lockers is like four-wheel-drive on steroids. It's also like trying to change the

direction of an out of control trailer truck. But lockers do allow you to ascend through terrain that might otherwise be impossible to climb. Unfortunately, the slow-and-easy upward crawl of four-wheel-drive is replaced by gunning it and a feeling of being out of control.

But lockers save the day here and on several other hills on this trail. On several of these slopes, I can feel the tendency of my bike to want to flip over backwards, and it's a very uncomfortable feeling. Leaning forward to shift my weight helps a lot. But with lockers engaged and nearly full throttle, leaning in any direction feels uncomfortable.

There are places with nearly level terrain where my lockers can be turned off, allowing slow trail navigation in four-wheel-drive. But many of the hairpin turns are best described as extremely "tipsy," due to the thick roots and boulders that border the trail. If there's anything worse than feeling like you're going over backwards, it's the feeling of going over sideways. Margy definitely wouldn't like this.

At times the trail flows effortlessly through fairly flat country where the path becomes little more than a swale to divert runoff, but also serves as an easy path to navigate on our quads.

We stop often to repair washed out areas and spots where big roots push into the trail (making for uneven and even unsafe navigation). Everyone has his own chainsaw, except me. Oh, I have a chainsaw, of course, but I forgot to bring it. On the evening before the ride, I stood in the room of my cabin where my tools are stored, and purposefully asked myself: "What tools can I bring to help out tomorrow?" In front of me were numerous implements, all pretty useless for trail repairs. Finally I decided to forgo bringing any tools, since John would share his with me. Right in front of me, sitting prominently on the floor but totally unnoticed, was my bright orange chainsaw.

I contribute a lot though, mostly with basic grunt work that's badly needed. While the other guys cut with their saws, I haul away the wood. And I use a pick-axe John has brought to dig out the high spots and redistribute the dirt. I do carry pruning shears that every quad rider needs to help get through alder infestations, and they prove useful in attacking the bushes and smaller roots along the sides of the trail.

Farther along, we stop bunched-up for a lunch break. We've come prepared for mosquitoes, but there are surprisingly almost none. By

the time we finish eating, the bugs have started to arrive, swirling around and occasionally necessitating a swat. But it's nothing like what you would expect in this marshy forest. Several small ponds, obvious mosquito breeding areas, sit off to the side of the trail where we take our break. But bugs have been adversely affected by the delayed arrival

of spring. This June's cool start indicates this might be another year without a summer, similar to the unusual conditions two years ago. Before we leave to begin work on the steep slope ahead, I dab on some insect repellant, but it seems hardly necessary.

In front of us is one of the biggest challenges of the day. Near the end of the trail, just before it dumps down onto flat and easily navigable terrain, is one of the worst sections. Here we find it necessary to completely change the direction of the trail for about 50 metres to avoid an eroded drop-off in a rocky area. In this section, chainsaws blare and I swing the axe and use my shears to cut the smaller stuff.

Blueberry roots are a particular problem. How can something so tasty in pies and tarts be such a mess when imbedded in a trail? A cluster of blueberry roots is enough to set a quad on its side in a tight turn.

A large tree root extends in all directions, framed on each side by giant blueberry mounds. The root includes a small stump, well decayed but still firmly imbedded in the center of what we've decided will be the new trail section. There's really no way around this spot, with steep inclines on both sides, so we have to tackle it. John and I hack at the root with axes, stopping occasionally so Mike and Jim can cut around the stump with their chainsaws. It's a matter of clearing

the area around the still-firm wood with the axes, then taking a chance with the chainsaw. There's lots of grit and small rocks in the soil. A single tiny rock is all it takes to destroy the blades of a chainsaw. But the saws somehow survive, though they are sometimes fully imbedded in the dirt as they cut.

When the stump finally seems a bit loose, Terry hooks up to it with his quad winch and hauls it out of the ground. The blueberry roots are nearly as challenging, but finally we're done and ready to test the descent with our quads.

"Still mighty steep," says Mike.

"Might be wise to go back through Heather Main," suggests Jim.

Even if the descent is acceptable, we'll still have to climb back up the same slope, and neither Jim nor Mike seem to like that prospect. Until now, I've been comfortable with returning the same way we came. The cautious remarks of two riders with much more experience makes me think twice. It's a long way back along Heather Main – including the new Theodosia trail I've heard described as "really tough." But even John seems to hesitate about coming back up this hill.

"Maybe we should all go back on Heather Main," he says. "Wayne hasn't seen the new Theo trail, so that would be interesting to him."

"Yes, interesting," I think to myself. But it sure sounds better than trying to return via the Last Chance Trail.

As usual, Terry is ready for whatever turns up, so he's quick to agree. I know his superior riding skills are tempered with an excellent attitude towards safety, so his immediate agreement is enough to seal the deal. We're taking the long way out.

*****

The ride out is long but enjoyable. Heather Main is an easy ride.

We come across some big cedars that have been cut and placed along the side of the road. John poses with one of the logs so I can get a photo with a sense of scale. What could these prize logs be doing here, with no other logging activity in sight?

Around the next corner, we find the answer. A bridge on the main is nearly washed out. Apparently, the big logs have been allocated to repair this structure. Talk about a bridge that will be rebuilt to skookum standards!

At the intersection where Heather Main joins Theodosia Main, we take a break from our ride. As we sit on our quads, engines off, a pickup truck rolls up in a cloud of dust. All of our trail crew (except me, of course) recognize the driver and passenger, two local loggers who are on their way home from Theodosia Valley. They'll need to drive all the way to Olsen's Landing on Powell Lake, then catch a crew boat back to the Shinglemill. As a logger, just getting to and from your worksite can absorb a big part of your day. But they still take time to gab with everyone for a few minutes. Then off they go again in another cloud of dust to catch their ride down the lake.

We continue down Theodosia Main along the bank of the inlet, now at low tide. As we roll through the winding industrial area near the logging dock, we pass the road that was briefly used by heavy trucks for entry into the valley. The wide, nearly-straight road is now piled high with dirt, completely impassible. Previously, a fairly challenging quad trail led into Theo. Then the logging company decided to build a new road to provide truck access. They logged from this road for a short time, then deactivated it. Such are the requirements when logging is complete. A logging road that's no longer needed is a financial burden to maintain. So when a logging company exits an area, the road is deactivated to prevent future liability. It's a big area of contention between logging companies (power companies, too) and local recreational users of the forests.

In this case, a nearly perfect road was destroyed by excavating equipment that dug deep trenches and piled boulders into high piles. Quad riders and hikers use only hand tools and chainsaws, so they have to live with the deactivations.

In many cases, such as this one, the original quad trail was destroyed in the process of building the new road. ATV riders often come in after roads are deactivated and try to make a new trail, as best as they can. In this case, the challenge was a big one. The new quad trail is passable, but just barely. It follows the original quad path in some sections, but mostly it's a new route. And what a route! – deep trenches in some places and steep slopes everywhere. For about 3 kilometres, the new trail is at the limits of my riding ability. I start counting the spots where Margy will feel uncomfortable. My count reaches "three" when we come to a place where even John has trouble. A deep trench causes him to roll back and make another try with lockers engaged. It's rare to see John fail at anything he attempts, so I know this trail is particularly outrageous. Following behind John, I have the advantage of watching where he places his wheels and how he applies the power. With this on my side, I make it though the trench on my first try, but just barely.

After exiting the new trail, we're back on the original road that heads out of Theodosia Valley. John stops at a new spur that leads off to the left and upward into a logging slash. I pull up behind him, and Mike and Jim follow behind me. Terry has been in front of us, and he's long gone.

"Have you been up there yet?" John asks Mike.

"Yes, it's an amazing view," replies Mike.

Jim nods in agreement. All but one of us has been there.

"Wayne hasn't seen this new viewpoint yet," says John. "So I'll take him up. You can get going back to your trucks. When you see Terry, tell him where we are."

John leads me up the winding stretch, an easy climb with only minor cross-trenches. We pull to a stop at the top, where the spur ends

in a wide, rocky clearing. Below us is a breathtaking view that looks to the north. We gaze down on Lancelot Inlet, the river-like connection into Theodosia, and out towards Tenedos Bay.

To the south, the view is just as spectacular – looking down on the islets that form the mouth of Okeover Inlet, across the Malaspina

Peninsula, and out to one of the islands beyond that's difficult to identify in the haze (either Cortes or Hernando). Vancouver Island is visible far in the distance.

Returning to the road, we continue out of Theodosia on the park-like trail that flows down the final big hill. This is one of my all-time favourite trails, winding through a beautiful forest grove. But it's also a bumpy and twisty ride that requires four-wheel drive. As usual, John takes Bro out of his box and makes him walk. He does it reluctantly, because the dog is dragging now, but it's a fairly short stretch.

I follow John's quad down, with Bro walking between us. From my viewpoint, Bro is trying to act brave, as if he still has plenty of energy. But I know he doesn't, and you can see it in his stumbling but determined gait.

At the bottom of the hill, John hoists Bro back into his box, and off we go for the last rough portion of the ride. "Rough" isn't an appropriate word after all we've seen today, but this is a rocky trail that leads upward towards the forest service road. Under normal conditions, I always consider it somewhat challenging. Today it's a piece of cake.

When we pull out onto the forest service road, John stops.

"I'm gonna' bring Bro up front with me," says John. "He was whining bad on that last stretch of trail."

"Up front? You mean on your lap?"

John nods: "Yes." I've never seen this before, but apparently it's not a first. I couldn't hear Bro whining over the noise of our engines, but I can imagine his pain.

John uses all of his muscles in both arms to lift the big dog and place him on his lap. Just getting seated on his quad is a struggle, but once in place, he's able to drive almost normally.

We're only a few kilometres from our trucks. I ride less than 10 metres behind John, and to his left. We're in a tight formation, but I'm in a position that keeps me out of the dust swirl from his Grizzly. It's a safe way to ride on a road like this, although I'm near the left shoulder. I keep a lookout for oncoming traffic and drop back when we approach a blind curve. When we hit a series of back-to-back turns, I drop back a full dust-length (about 50 metres) behind John.

It's been quite a round-trip. We haven't retraced a single portion of road. Here, on our last leg of the trip, the bright yellow signs again mark our kilometre progress in distinct black (and misspelled) letters: "Thedosia Forest Service Road, Branch 2."

Epilogue

Outdoors

After nearly a decade in the region, I'm finally able to experience Powell Lake in all seasons. I still spend time in the States, but it's seldom more than a few days at a time. I live on the lake full-time and have nearly unlimited opportunities to explore the backcountry on my quad.

But to climb onto my quad, I must leave the lake. That's not so easy these days. I love Powell Lake so much that any time away seems like punishment, unless I can justify it for multiple reasons. So usually, my rides up the main are accompanied by a trip to town for book business, a meeting, or at least a grocery run.

Are you like that? Do you sometimes avoid things you hold dear (a quad ride, a boat trip, even a vacation) because you are so comfortable in your home? Are you also like me in what happens when you do take the plunge? Isn't the quad ride (or the golf match, or the hockey game) always worth the sacrifice? Once I'm on the trail, I'm "at home" with the environment and thrilled I took the time to hook up the quad trailer. Sometimes, just getting moving is all that's required.

Getting outdoors has always been a cure for some of the heaviest concerns in life. When you're there, your anxieties evaporate. The closer you get to nature, in your own personal way, the quicker the cure. Quad riding (or hiking, or kayaking) can make a considerable dent in our personal health, if only we can get started.

And the best news of all for me – when the ride is complete, I get to go back up the lake. We all get to go home, and get ready for the next ride.

For those of us in Coastal BC who are privileged by a sublime environment, we only need to step outside and head uphill. The trails are peaceful and remote, and among the most beautiful in the world. Ride, or hike, or bike. Just get started. You'll never regret the trip.

Geographic Index

Alaska Pine   p.18 - 21, 186
Appleton Creek   p.87 - 93, 194
Beartooth Mountain   p.25
Big Tree (near Mount Alfred)   p.45 - 47, 64
Blue Ridge   p.24, 107
Bunster Range   p.74 - 75, 85, 89 - 90, 111. 113, 120. 193 - 194
Chippewa Lake (in Bunster Range)   p.89
Chippewa Bay (on Powell Lake)   p.13, 111 - 113, 117, 120- 124, 188, 194
Dalgleish Main   p.167
D-Branch   p. 34, 37, 63, 69
Dianne Main   p.37
Dodd Lake   p.33, 105, 151
Duck Lake   p.17, 41, 145, 153,
Eldred River   p.35 - 37
Fiddlehead Farm (Powell Lake)   p.95 - 97, 102 - 103
Freda Creek   p.135
Freda Mountain   p.135
Giovanno Lake (Giovanni Lake, Frog Lake)   p.101, 104
Giovanno Lake Main (Giovanni Lake Main)   p.100 - 101
Goat Island (Goat Mountain)   p.16, 25, 78
Goat Lake   p.27, 34 - 36, 151
Goat Lake Main (Goat Main, Weldwood Main)   p.31, 34, 37, 97- 98, 105 - 106, 133 - 134, 138, 154
Good Hope Trail   p.132, 142 - 143
Gordon Pasha Lake (Pasha Lake)   p.132
Granite Lake   p.84 - 85
Granite Lake Main   p.147
Granite Lake 6   p.144 , 147 - 149, 114
Haslam Lake   p.16 - 18, 24 - 25, 97, 101, 107, 127, 145
Heather Main   p.79, 110 - 112, 116 - 122, 127 - 132, 200 - 201
Hole in the Wall (Powell Lake)   p.12 - 14, 69, 111 - 112, 122 - 123, 172, 188 - 189, 195
Ice Lake   p.27 - 28, 41, 45 - 50, 63 - 64

Geographic Index

Khartoum Lake (Third Lake)   p.132 - 135, 139, 141
Khartoum Lake Main (Third Lake Main)   p.132, 136
Knuckleheads   p.135
Larson's Landing   p.115
Last Chance Trail   p.75, 91, 111 - 113, 120, 123, 186, 188,
      194 - 195, 200
Lewis Lake   p.98 - 100
Lewis Lake Main   p.98 - 99
Lois Lake   p.31, 132 - 133, 135, 139
Lois River   p.141, 183
Mount Alfred   p.27, 38, 43 - 44, 46, 50, 63 - 64, 69, 95
Mount Mahony   p.25, 84 - 86, 101, 107, 177
Okeover Inlet   p.46, 74, 80, 90, 194, 203
Olsen's Creek (Olsen Creek)   p.168, 170
Olsen's Landing   p.161, 163 - 164, 168, 201
Olsen's Lake (Olsen Lake)   p.78, 156. 160 - 161, 170, 175 - 176
Olsen's Main (Olsen Lake Main)   p.165
Rainbow Main   p.34, 105
Rupert's Farm (Palmer Farm)   p.77, 80, 108, 129, 131
Sliammon Lake   p.87 - 90, 93
Southview Road   p.72, 115, 158, 190 - 193
Spring Lake   p.100
Spring Lake Main   p.98
Sunshine Coast Trail (SCT)   p.93, 100, 115, 147, 151
Theodosia Inlet   p76, 79 - 81, 108, 131, 203
Theodosia Main (Theodosia Valley Main)   p.76, 79 -80, 129, 201
Theodosia River   p.78, 131, 108
Theodosia Valley   p.67, 70, 73 - 76, 79, 108 - 109, 111, 115,
      127 - 128, 131, 160, 188, 200 - 202, 204
Tin Hat Junction   p31, 98, 134 - 135
Tin Hat Mountain   p.25, 98
Walt Hill (Tower Hill, Radio Hill)   p.146, 151
Wilde Road   p.85, 93
Windsor Lake   p.29. 32. 105. 151

About the Author

Author interviewing Bro on his quad in Theodosia Valley

From 1980 to 2005, Wayne Lutz was Chairman of the Aeronautics Department at Mount San Antonio College in Los Angeles. He has also served 20 years as a U.S. Air Force C-130 aircraft maintenance officer. His educational background includes a B.S. degree in physics from the University of Buffalo and an M.S. in systems management from the University of Southern California. The author is a flight instructor with 7000 hours of flying experience.

For the past three decades, he has spent summers in Canada, exploring remote regions in his Piper Arrow, camping next to his airplane. The author now resides in a floating cabin on Canada's Powell Lake in all seasons, and occasionally in a city-folk condo in Bellingham, Washington. His writing genres include regional Canadian publications and science fiction.

Science Fiction Novels
by
Wayne J. Lutz

Inbound to Earth
Wayne J. Lutz

Echo of a Distant Planet
Wayne J. Lutz

www.PowellRiverBooks.com

Farther Up the Main is the 7th in a series of volumes focusing on the unique places and memorable people of coastal British Columbia

Order at:
www.PowellRiverBooks.com

Coastal BC Living Blog
PowellRiverBooks.blogspot.com